Revivals

OF ANTIGONE

WILLIAM ROBERT

Published by State University of New York Press, Albany

© 2015 State University of New York

All rights reserved

Printed in the United States of America

No part of this book may be used or reproduced in any manner whatsoever without written permission. No part of this book may be stored in a retrieval system or transmitted in any form or by any means including electronic, electrostatic, magnetic tape, mechanical, photocopying, recording, or otherwise without the prior permission in writing of the publisher.

For information, contact State University of New York Press, Albany, NY
www.sunypress.edu

Production, Eileen Nizer
Marketing, Anne M. Valentine

Library of Congress Cataloging-in-Publication Data

Robert, William, 1974–
  Revivals: of Antigone / William Robert.
      pages cm
  Includes bibliographical references and index.
  ISBN 978-1-4384-5801-4 (hardcover : alk. paper)
  ISBN 978-1-4384-5802-1 (paperback : alk. paper)
  ISBN 978-1-4384-5803-8 (e-book)
  1. Antigone (Mythological character)   I. Title.

BL820.A68R63 2015
292.2'13—dc23   2014043289

10 9 8 7 6 5 4 3 2 1

To my families

"Let's face it. We're undone by each other. And if we're not, we're missing something."

— Judith Butler

Contents

Present / ix

Previval / xi

First Revival: Antigone the Animal / 1

Second Revival: Antigone the Angel / 33

Third Revival: Antigone the Future / 59

Notes / 71

Bibliography of Works Cited and Consulted / 85

Index / 97

Present

This text didn't exist. Then I found it.

I found it thanks to an invitation, to send without worrying about arrival. I didn't know I had a response until I received the invitation. There wasn't a text to look for until I thought to look for it.

What I found was familiarly strange. It was a lost letter I'd never written. Having discovered it, I posted it, into print. It's the text you're reading.

I would not have found this text I hadn't lost if I hadn't received another invitation, from the Luce Irigaray Circle, to present work at its 2013 conference. For their encouraging comments and helpful critiques, I thank Per Buvik, Sara Heinämaa, Timothy Johnston, Danae McLeod, Britt-Marie Schiller, and Gail Schwab.

I would not have known where to look for this lost-and-found text without the perceptive care of Michael Miller. His insight and sensitivity to signifiers enabled me to see this text, and to see what it is about. I remain grateful to him.

I would not have found this text without the simple advice of Verlyn Klinkenborg. I remain thankful for his words.

I would not have dared to find and then send this text without the incredible grace and unbounded friendship of Virginia Burrus. It was amid letters we sent to one another that I thought to look for this text and, once discovered, to send it. I remain indebted to her.

I would not have found a place to send this text from without Syracuse University's Department of Religion. I remain obliged for their ongoing support and for their subvention of this work.

I would not have been able to send this text without the perspectives and efforts of Andrew Kenyon and Mary-Jane Rubenstein. I remain appreciative of their guidance and of SUNY Press's backing.

I would not have imagined or risked, lost or found, discovered or disseminated, this little book without my families. They have sent affection and compassion and loving kindness—and then generously resent them when I misplaced their packages of care. Their gifts have been reviving.

To them I send my gratitude and love, and this text, as a thank-you note and an IOU. Addressees include Jonalyn and Raoul, Shelby and Jon, Noah and Josephine, Lucas and Leah, as well as Zoran and Charlie, Tom and Roger, Elisabeth and Karmen, Beth and Jacob, John and Jack, Pat and David, Gareth and Marcia, Nell and Ellen.

I hope this sending finds you.

Previval

> It's really important to get somehow into the mind and make it move somewhere it has never moved before. That happens partly because the material is mysterious or unknown but mostly because of the way you push the material around from word to word in a sentence. . . . Given whatever material we're going to talk about, and we all know what it is, how can we move within it in a way we've never moved before, mentally? That seems like the most exciting thing to do with your head.
>
> — Anne Carson

I thought I was done with Antigone. I have taught courses about her. I have given conference papers about her. I have written articles and a book about her. After all of that, after being together for more than a decade, I thought I was finished with her.

I was wrong.

I am not done with her. Or she is not done with me—with us. She, it seems, returns like the repressed, as powerfully and as predictably. She perdures and endures, insists and persists. After nearly 2,500 years, she keeps coming back, or we keep coming back to her, each time with a new question. She persists as a question, one that insists, calls for response.

Why? Why, after millennia of rereading, does Antigone keep returning? Why does she continue to call for revivals?

And why respond? Why revive Antigone? More pressingly, why revive Antigone now?

I don't have an answer to any of these opening questions. I don't have *an* answer. I have many, potential answers. But (full disclosure upfront) none will ultimately answer any of these questions, not completely, not once and for all. Antigone insists and persists—and resists closure. She is not an answer. She is a question. She remains in question.

She remains *poly*: many, multiple. (She, like Walt Whitman, contains multitudes.)[1] She is polytheistic, revering multiple gods. She is polysemic, meaning multiply, even excessively. She means too much. She is polyphasic and polyvalent, occurring in multiple stages and combining many things. She is polymorphic and polymorphous, coming in many forms and remaining formative, in formation. She is even, to borrow Sigmund Freud's phrase, polymorphously perverse. She is polysexual, performing masculinity as well as multiple femininities. She is polyzoontic, a neologism that enfolds *poly*, *zōē*, *zōon*, and *ontic*: plurality, living, being.

Antigone is polygraphic. A polygraph is a machine that measures vital signs, such as heart rate (and hence blood flow), as a means of discerning truth. A polygraph interprets vitality as a way of interpreting, determining, assigning validity. Antigone performs this polygraphic operation, diagnosing or deciding on what is valid based on what is vital.

She is also etymologically poly-graphic. She engenders poly-graphics: multi-writing(s). These poly-graphics call for a *poly* hermeneutics, pursuing many expositional paths and accommodating multiple interpretations—and reinterpretations. These expositional paths cross disciplinary terrains. They induce reinterpretations that are philological, philosophical, psychological, political, historical, cultural, dramaturgical, sexual, religious, or some combination of these.[2]

These rereadings, reinterpretations, are *poly*: many and multiple—too many, too multiple, to count. And they continue to come. With every re-turn, Antigone re-calls for re-readings.

Each return brings a reinterpretation. Each revival recasts Antigone. After more than two millennia, she has acquired quite a repertoire of roles. She is polyperformative, cast and recast in so many roles, in so many contexts. Antigone has performed as feminist and antifeminist, humanist and antihumanist, human and inhuman, masculine and feminine, defiant and cooperative, aristocratic and democratic, sovereignty-usurping and sovereignty-rejecting, death-desiring and life-loving. These reviving, often conflicting, recastings indicate her persisting relevance.

(In the last two centuries, Antigone's revivals recur with greater frequency. They have resulted in what some have called an Antigone effect, and even Antigone fever.)

Some of her most notable roles come from castings by modern philosophical master-minds. She plays a dialectically sublated sister for G. W. F. Hegel and an exemplarily homeless human for Martin Heidegger. For Jacques Lacan, she portrays an ethical extreme who lives in "unbearable splendor" between two deaths. Jacques Derrida casts her as "the system's vomit." Under Judith Butler's direction, she performs a gender-troubling, kinship-destabilizing "occasion for a new field of the human."³

Among these stagings, only Hegel's locates Antigone. Only Hegel's puts Antigone in her place: the *oikos*, the place of "womankind" (*Weiblichkeit*). In Hegel's mise-en-scène, Antigone stays at home, in the dark. On these other stages, Antigone does not stay anywhere. She is dislocated and dislocating: homeless (Heidegger), excessive (Lacan), undigestible (Derrida), inhuman (Butler).

Luce Irigaray dislocates Antigone again—and again. She repeatedly recasts Antigone (especially Hegel's Antigone) throughout her textual corpus, from 1974's *Speculum of the Other Woman* through 2013's *In the Beginning, She Was* (a title that seems apropos of Antigone). Between these texts come other recastings, in *This Sex Which Is Not One*, *An Ethics of Sexual Difference*, *Sexes and Genealogies*, *Thinking the Difference*, *I Love to You*, and *To Be Two*.

Antigone's reappearances in these texts are not simple repetitions. Irigaray creatively recasts Antigone in a variety of roles, but without relinquishing or erasing her prior castings of Antigone. These castings include as an unsettling sister; as a respectful subject of earthly and cosmic orders, of the dead and the divine; as a key ancestor in engendering feminine genealogies; as a lover of life; and as an enduring example (whether model or warning) for women.

In Irigaray's mise-en-scène, Antigone enacts these roles, each resolutely feminine, on sexual difference's stages of ontology, genealogy, and ethics. Antigone's enduring relevance means that Antigone repeatedly returns to these stages. In revival after revival, Antigone replays her roles—or plays new ones. She is not yet offstage. Ontology, genealogy, and ethics are not done with Antigone, either.

Nor will they be, according to Irigaray. Antigone's example, she writes, "is always to be meditated upon as a figure of History and as an identity or identification for many young girls or women living today" (and, I would add, not only for girls and women).[4] Irigaray exemplifies her exhortation. She will, she writes, repeatedly "return, once again, to the figure of Antigone because of her relevance [à cause de son actualité]," with each return "reviving the message of Antigone and pursuing its embodiment in our culture."[5]

Just as Antigone keeps coming back, Irigaray keeps coming back to Antigone. Irigaray keeps returning to Antigone. She keeps reviving Antigone and her message by recasting her, again and again, in this range of roles.

But what if Antigone played other roles?

The text that follows turns on this question. It unfolds as an extended response to this question.

This question contains or engenders other questions. Why might Antigone play other roles? What other roles might she play? In what other ways might she be cast? What effects might her playing other roles have?

These dramatic questions are also ethical questions. They are *other* questions: questions of otherness, alterity, disparity, divergence, difference, even differance. They ask, dramatically: What roles other than those she already plays might Antigone play? They also ask, ethically: What roles of others, of animated otherness, might Antigone play? She plays an other, always a sexuate other, in many of her repertorial roles: feminine, sororal, homeless, excessive, undigestible, inhuman, as well as respectful, ancestral, exemplary. She performs disruptive differences that desire real differentiation.

Real differentiation requires, in each case, a real, robust difference. It requires more than being an other defined as a lesser version of a single, monolithic ideal. It requires being other than a not-A (or not-quite-A) to an ideal A. A not-A, which Irigaray calls an "other of the same," is a reductive, hierarchically devalued, illusory other. A not-A is a merely mimetic mirror image.

Antigone is no mere mirror image. She does not act as an other of the same. She enacts an *other* other. In doing so, she performs robust alterities, irreducible differences.

She performs them from the start. Her differences are sexual, familial, filial, religious, legal, political, and biological.

Antigone and her siblings (her brothers, Eteokles and Polyneikes, and her sister, Ismene) are children of an incestuous union, between Oedipus and Jokasta. She insists on these kinship bonds, and on her piety, by insisting on doing her divinely ordained sisterly duty: to bury Polyneikes's dead body (twice). By doing so, she transgresses the edict of Kreon, her uncle and Thebes's king, forbidding Polyneikes's burial. Antigone acts according to laws other than Kreon's. Her act and her refusal to repent for it render her politically other. They ultimately render her biotically other, when (as her punishment) Kreon has her buried alive. Left to die, she instead hangs herself in her tomb. Her suicide engenders the suicides of Haimon, Kreon's son and Antigone's fiancé, and then of Eurydike, Kreon's wife.

Antigone's *other* performances insist ethically. She, Irigaray writes, "asks [demande] to be considered as really an other, irreducible to the masculine subject" or any related hommology.[6] She calls for other relations, with real others.

So, what if Antigone played *other* roles? What if Antigone played roles of *other* others? What other roles of otherness might she perform? What other others might she portray, or become?

To respond to these other questions, I stage three revivals of Antigone. These revivals are not reprisals. They do not mount new versions of old productions. To do so would occasion reproductions rather than revivals. Such reproductions would be more imitative than imaginative, more mimetic than poetic. I suggest something different: three other revivals, of other Antigones. I recast Antigone as an animal, an angel, and a future.

By responding to these other questions, I respond to my opening question: why revive Antigone, and why now? Recasting Antigone in other roles shows her enduring relevance, now. It evinces her *poly*-ness. It intimates why she keeps returning, persisting, calling for revival.

Why revive Antigone now? Because she can intervene now as never before. Particularly recast in these other roles, Antigone can intervene in "the human" and in the humanities.

She intervenes at the edges. Antigone tests "the human": its pliability, its mutability, its boundary. In her other recastings, Antigone presses the human. She presses on the human. She pushes it to its limits, seeing how far it will go, how long it will last, before fracturing.

In doing so, she unearths its limits' past movements. These human limits have moved before, expanding from their androcentric delimitations to include differences. These differences, these others, include—at least ostensibly, nominally—women (sexual others), ethnicities ("racial" and genealogical others), slaves (social and financial others). They include primitives (cultural and religious others) and degenerates (mental and moral others). They include cyborgs (mechanical and organic others) and zombies (mortal and medical others) and many other others. This list is necessarily incomplete because these human limits remain on the move.

How far will they move? Reviving Antigone offers a way of seeing. Her revivals have tracked these moves. Antigone has been cast as almost every one of these others. She has been and is cast as inhuman.

This casting is nothing new. It is part of the original casting, the original staging, by Sophokles in 442 BCE. When Antigone makes her first public appearance in the play that bears her name, the chorus greets her by calling her "monstrous [*teras*]."[7] This interjection immediately follows the choral Ode to Man, a hymn to humanism—the first in occidental literature. Having just established and extolled the human, the chorus encounters Antigone and cries "inhuman." (The chorus names Antigone negatively, as not human.)

My revivals of Antigone as animal, angel, and future also cast Antigone as inhuman. But they name "inhuman" positively, specifically: as "other than human," not "less than human"; as *alter*, not *sub*. They ascribe Antigone identities rather than refusing her one. These inhuman identities push against human borders, portending potential border breeches. As animal, angel, and future, Antigone tests the human from the *other* side.

By testing the human, Antigone tests humanism. She is a test case for humanism's resilience and renaissance, however maximal or minimal, however muscular or meek. Her testing revivals reveal humanism's current contours, its contemporary challenges. They uncover humanism's relations to its resistant, dis-ordering offspring: antihumanism, transhumanism, posthumanism. They test for what "human" names *now*, and for what others remain unnamed.

Her "human" interventions, through her "inhuman" revivals, intervene in the humanities. They cross disciplinary boundaries. They mix methods. They join conversations about animals, religions, sexualities, biopolitics. They interlace these fields of critical inquiry. They interpose phenomenological, ethical, and ontological queries.

The revivals that I stage here can help to revive the humanities. They can recall their vitality, their import, for shaping and reshaping real relations, reflexive and reciprocal, with humans and with others. Other Antigones make way for other humanities, for other human-animal and human-divine relations. Other Antigones engender other sexualities, and other sexual differences. Other Antigones herald other ways of reading Antigone and other ways of reading others *through* Antigone.

Her revivals' human and humanistic effects recall my opening double question (why revive Antigone, now?) by responding to it: because Antigone is undone. She returns, calls for revivals, remains, because she remains undone. She is, still, undone. She is, still, unmastered, untamed, unconfined, untied, unfinished. She is unbounded and unbinding.

Antigone remains loose, on the loose, loosening. She loosens. She loose-ends. Antigone is a loose(ning) woman. She undoes. She is undone because she is, still, undoing. Loose-ending, unbinding, undoing are her effects. They are the effects of her interventions. They are what her revivals perform.

To stage these revivals, to unfold these other recastings, I offer something a bit loose. I tender something loosened, or loosen(d)ed. I venture something unbinding and unbounded. In doing so, I resound Irigaray's methodological disclosure, that "what I am going to say to you, or confide in you, today, will remain rather primary, loose [*délié*]. Deliberately [*délibérément*], and also time's fault. . . . So I will speak more or less freely [*librement*], offering, to your associations or interpretations, some of my experiences, trials, associations, still nocturnal or oneiric."[8]

"Loose" does not mean lax or lacking care. "Loose," "*délié*," means not tied up. It means not "tied up," as in a scene of bondage. "Loose" means unmastered, untamed, unvanquished. It also means not "tied up" as a package or a present or a totality would be. "Loose" means undone. It means to still have loose ends.

I have not tied up all the loose ends. I have left many undone. I have left open questions, as potential places for further exploration. Loose ends abound in my experiences, trials, associations of Antigone.

What follows, woven of these experiences, trials, associations, is an essay about Antigone. It is an essay about otherness, about other kinds of others, about how others count according to human valuative metrics. It is an essay about ontology and ethics, entwined.

What follows is an essay: an attempt, an experience, a trial, a venture, an adventure. It is unconventional. It ventures to forego some scholarly protocols, such as reviews of secondary literatures done for their own sakes. It does not have a footnote fetish. It does not wade into the tide pools of internecine academic skirmishes.

It does not announce, or take, an "Antigonean turn," akin to so many scholarly turns: linguistic, pictorial, material, corporeal, affective, performative, postmodern, posthuman, animal, global, biopolitical, ethical, ontological, and undoubtedly others. (We need not "turn" to Antigone. She will return to us.) It does not explicitly address "Antigone studies" (which, to my horror, exists) or attempt to turn Antigone into one more "area" of studies.

I refuse to turn Antigone into an adjective. She is no modifier. She remains a proper name, which resounds. (I might consider turning Antigone into a verb if I could know what "to Antigone" might mean, what this Antigone-action would be or do—since Antigone does so many things . . .)

What follows is an essay. It is imaginative—inventive, innovative, excentric, definitely queer, potentially idiosyncratic, possibly zany. It is imaginative, which means it is not primarily exegetical or commentarial. It asks not "what is?" but "what if?" It turns on an imaginative question. It takes a leap, speculates. It remains loose, and it loosen(d)s. It is a risk. It is, in Irigaray's words, a "risk that risks life itself. Exceeding it barely by a breath."[9] It undertakes the risk of a revival, a revitalization, maybe even a kind of resurrection.

In undertaking this risk, this excentric venture, I take my cue from a passage of Irigaray's: "to stage the stakes of this work, I will once again take the figure of Antigone as my point of departure [*pour mettre en scène l'enjeu du travail, je repartirai de la figure d'Antigone*]."[10] This essay is, in many ways, a sustained rereading of this passage. It is a performance of this passage—a passage of revivals: of returning, restarting, departing again. (There is, interestingly, no such thing as a "vival." There is only a *re*vival.) Each of the revivals that I stage takes Antigone as its point of departure. Each revival departs, once again, from Antigone. Departing again is also departing from: a difference or deviation, an other route.

Each risky revival of Antigone redeparts from her by staging a conversation. Each conversation engages different discourses, different subjects, different conversation partners. Across all three conversations, Irigaray remains my principal interlocutor. My revivals of Antigone recast her in other, potential, Irigarayan roles: animal, angel, future. These revivals become double revivals: of Antigone and Irigaray, each through the other. Their revivals open both to possible (and, remember, rather loose) recastings, rereadings, re-visions. They open new hermeneutic paths for following, or pursuing, Antigone and Irigaray.

Why revive Antigone now? Because doing so by way of Irigaray presents new revivals, new recastings, new imaginative possibilities for Antigone. And we need them. As Bonnie Honig writes, "we need a new Antigone."[11] We need new Antigones, in the plural. We need, Honig writes, "to pluralize Antigone, develop new readings, incite new performances," through which she "is re-birthed by later receptions and alien contexts."[12] We need new, other Antigones.

Responding to this call for a new Antigone, or new Antigones, means that I do not stage a mere reprisal of Irigaray's Antigone(s). Such a reprisal would replicate a sequence of scenes. It would involve set pieces—condensed, digested, reductive repetitions—from Irigaray's readings of Antigone. Scene 1: "The Eternal Irony of the Community." Scene 2: "An Ethics of Sexual Difference." Scene 3: "The Forgotten Mystery of Female Ancestry." Scene 4: "She Before the King." And so on.

These double revivals revitalize Antigone through Irigaray—and Irigaray through Antigone. Irigaray offers other ways of recasting Antigone. Antigone, in turn, offers new ways of rereading Irigaray. Together, they make way for imagining new figurations of human-nonhuman (human-animal and human-divine) distinctions and relations.

These new figurations come between. They arrive in *between* spaces, and through *between* figures, of Antigone and Irigaray: an animal (between human and nonhuman), an angel (between human and divine), an awaited event (between now and then). These refiguring relations are *between* relations. They are *inter*: *inter alios*, *inter modos*, *inter vitas*, *inter naturas*. They are *inter*-active. They happen in thresholds. They loosen(d) in between.

They loosen(d) by questioning. Redepartures from Antigone proceed through questions: this essay's opening question (Why revive Antigone, now?) and its pivotal question (What if Antigone played other roles?). Responding to these questions restages "the stakes of this work"—which are vital. Why revive and recast Antigone? Because doing so discloses new ontological and ethical conceptions of life and the living.

These conceptions follow from variations on a valuative question: who or what "counts," and how? What counts as life? What counts as human? Who counts as human? Who else counts? Who (else) counts as a who? Who counts among the living? How much do they count? How might their counting recount "us"?

These are living questions. They are vital. They, like Antigone, persist, insist, call for response.

"To stage the stakes of this work, I will once again take the figure of Antigone as my point of departure."[13] I depart, once again, from Antigone. I depart from other Antigones, to stage *other* revivals.

I am definitely not done with her.

First Revival
Antigone the Animal

> What animal? The other.
> — Jacques Derrida

> To stage the stakes of this work, I will once again take the figure of Antigone as my point of departure.
> — Luce Irigaray

Antigone is out for blood.

Antigone is all about blood. Blood motivates and mobilizes her allegiances and actions. It forms the substance of her bonds with others. These bonds overflow mortal borders—borders that blood demarcates. They bind Antigone to the living (those in whom blood still flows) and the dead (those in whom blood no longer flows). Life and death are matters of blood and its flow.

These bonds also overflow human borders. They bind Antigone to the human and the nonhuman. Antigone's blood flows over these and other borders, flooding divisions of nature and culture.

These divisions are cultural. "Nature" is cultural. It is a cultural fabrication. Nature exists only in terms of, in relation to, a culture—a human culture. A culture makes nature an "other of the same," an illusory other against which it delineates itself. Nature is a culture's incorporated other: grafted, digested, domesticated.

Nature is a human name for otherness—for living otherness, for organic others.[1] "Nature" frequently names "nonhuman," whether animal, vegetal, viral, bacterial, or otherwise. In these (and most other) cases, nonhuman means subhuman: less than human, according to humanistic hierarchical values. Humanism appraises "human" as intrinsically more valuable than "nonhuman." This greater value justifies human cultural conquests of nature. Impelled by humanism, (human) culture tramples, tames, domesticates, dominates (nonhuman) nature.

Nature is a humanistic name for what humans master and overcome. It is a humanistic excuse, and rallying cry, for this masterful overcoming.

This rallying cry is initially exclaimed in Sophokles's *Antigone*. It comes in the play's first choral song (or *stasimon*), known as the Ode to Man (lines 332–75). This hymn to humanism lauds humans' subjugation of anything nonhuman. Subjects of such subjugation include earth, nonhuman animals, and gods: "the highest of gods he wears away, / the tireless immortal Earth [*Gaia*]"; "the tribes of light-headed birds, / all kinds of savage beasts, / and creatures born in the salty sea, / he traps with his intricate coiling nets / and leads away—ingenious man!"[2] And it is *man* (*anēr*). Humanism is sexed from the start. It is hommosexual: markedly sexed, and sexed masculine. Humanism is hommohumanism. For humanism, human becomes hu*man*.

Women, like nonhuman animals (and others), get trapped in his nets. Women are, specifically, netted together with birds, beasts, and fish. They get subsumed into nature, and then domesticated. Women, like nonhuman animals, are named "nature," by men's "culture." Women, like nonhuman animals, become "others of the same." In these and related ways, women and nonhuman animals are akin, naturally, as Antigone illustrates. (Women's kinship with birds is particularly significant for Antigone, and in *Antigone*.)

Nature is a humanistic name for otherness, for difference. This difference includes sexual difference, which streams through "nature" and "culture." Sexual difference precedes their nominations. It comes before them. It flows through them, or they flow through it. It serves as a kind of life-blood.

Nature and culture are humanistic, and so sexual, names. They valuate differences according to a humanistic metric. This metric is sexualized, since sexual difference is a fluid foundation of humanism—which is to say, culture.

Sexual difference is a vital, founding fluid (or fluidity) that courses through nature and culture. It is founding, Luce Irigaray writes, "because it is the most basic and universal [difference], the one which first articulates nature and culture."[3]

Sexual difference is an inescapable difference. There is no getting around sexual difference. It is *an* originary, ontological, natural or cultural difference, one that precedes "nature" and "culture" (and nonhuman-human). It is not *the* originary, ontological, natural or cultural difference.

Sexual difference is not *a* difference. It is differences. Sexual difference does not delimit only masculine and feminine.[4] It does that, but not only that. Neither masculine nor feminine is monolithic. They are pluralities. There are masculinities and femininities. Masculinities and femininities name ways of being, ways of living, ways of embodying, ways of desiring, ways of acting, ways of reacting, ways of relating. Sexual difference delimits these differences, too.

Sexual difference is always sexual differences. It has to be. To have or make a difference is to have or make differences. Difference is always in the plural. Difference is always differences. To mark this plurality, I write difference(s).

(Avowing difference as a plural means that there can be no first difference. Any first difference would already demarcate differences. This avowal marks a pivotal difference—pivotal differences—between Irigaray's and my ways of proceeding. It does not mark a permanent parting of ways. It marks a loosen[d]ing, not an untethering. It marks a break, not a breakup.)

(Avowing difference as a plural, as difference[s], means avowing plurality rather than multiplicity. Plurality maintains differences. Multiplicity often collapses differences into a differential multiplex. This multiplex is so complex, or convoluted, that its differences become virtually undifferentiated. It risks making "difference" transcendental. This risk is perilous. It seems too risky. Why? Because *differences count*.)

There is no real rupture, then, between nature and culture. They are not nature/culture, kept separate by a slash. They are not abyssally apart. Nor are they melded, dissolved without distinction. They are not natureculture, mixed hommogeneously. Nature and culture are inseparable, flowing. But inseparability and interflow do not mean sameness. Nature and culture are chiastic, or chiasmatic. They are nature-culture, with a hyphen between that grafts, but spaces, them. This hyphen preserves difference(s) and movement.

Blood flows through this hyphen as through a vein. Blood is the fluid, and fluidity, of nature-culture. Nature and culture, like life and death, are matters of blood and its flow.

So is language. Language, Irigaray writes, "however formal it might be, is nourished by blood, by flesh, by material elements."[5] Language and other symbolic orders remain bound to blood. They depend on materiality, especially corporeality.

Kinship is one symbolic system that, like language, is blood-bound. Some structural humanisms (including anthropology and psychoanalysis) try to unbind kinship from blood. Kinship, they insist, is wholly symbolic. Its founding prohibition of incest, on their accounts, transcends nature (and "natural" materiality) and inaugurates culture, which bears immaterial symbolic systems. Culture becomes a matter of immaterial symbols. Kinship, Judith Butler writes, then "ceases to be thought in terms of blood relations or naturalized social arrangements but becomes the effect of a linguistic set of relations" and exchanges.[6] Kinship becomes dematerialized.

How can it? Grounding kinship structures and exchanges is the prohibition of incest. This prohibition is a prohibition of blood: of consanguinity. Consanguinity hinges on familial proximity. To cross, or crisscross, overly proximate bloodlines (such as those of siblings) is to cross the line of incest. It is to cross the humanistic line demarcating human from subhuman, culture from nature. It is to behave like a "natural," nonhuman animal. Such behavior confuses, or transfuses, kinship roles. A father, for example, can be also a brother.

This example uncovers incest's ultimate "danger": reproduction. Incestuous procreation permanently confounds kinship's rules and roles. It does so materially, in a living child's body and blood. Incest lives on in this child's blood and bloodline. Incest's real threat to kinship remains material and corporeal.

Antigone and her siblings realize this threatening materiality. With them, Irigaray writes, "blood is already no longer pure."[7] Their father-brother, Oedipus, is unconscious of his kinship with their (and his) mother, Jokasta. Oedipus and Jokasta do not see the signs of kinship. But they disrupt kinship nonetheless: by procreating. Incestuous desire disturbs kinship. Incestuous reproduction devastates kinship. (Incestuous desire troubles kinship because it might lead to incestuous procreation.)

Kinship structures, and so their prohibition of incest, are human and humanistic products. They are creations of cultures. But they remain rooted in living materiality. They remain bloody.

(I am not suggesting that kinship is not symbolic. It is. I am suggesting that kinship is not only, not wholly, symbolic. I am suggesting that for kinship, materiality matters.)

Emphasizing reproduction emphasizes paternity and maternity, as permanent, material markers—of blood. Kinship requires perpetuation, which requires procreation, drawing blood into lines. In kinship terms, paternity and maternity map onto masculine and feminine. Sexualities become (fixed) functions, not (fluid) identities. Masculinity becomes paternal-masculine, and femininity becomes maternal-feminine—in those orders. But those orders bleed together. They are no longer separate or separable, by a hyphen. They become paternalmasculine and maternalfeminine—or, perhaps, paternal(masculine) and maternal(feminine).

(Why no hyphen, no spacing? To signal that there is no space to move, no room to breathe.)

These functional sexualities become heteronormative, and heteronormatively (re)productive. They work for kinship.[8]

They also become humanistically hierarchized. The paternalmasculine aligns with culture, which he creates and controls—and uses to control nature, which he aligns with the maternalfeminine. She becomes associated with materiality (as opposed to ideality), with fluid (as opposed to solid), with blood (as opposed to bloodlines), with procreation (as opposed to creation), with unconsciousness (as opposed to consciousness). These associations occur because of the impossibility of differentiating maternal and feminine. For the paternalmasculine, there is no difference, no space, no room to breathe, between maternal and feminine. The maternalfeminine remains repressed in this lack of difference. She, maternalfeminine, becomes a function of him, paternalmasculine. She is literally domesticated: kept at home (*oikos*), and in the dark.

Humanistic sexuality becomes hommosexuality. In terms of blood and bloodlines, consanguinity becomes hommosanguinity.[9]

Still, she, an "other of the same," feeds him. "Re-semblance," Irigaray writes, "cannot do without red blood. Mother-matter-nature must still and always nourish speculation."[10] The paternalmasculine feeds on the maternalfeminine's blood as if it were milk, as if he were her child.

Her fluid doubles. It transubstantiates, into blood and milk. The maternalfeminine becomes doubly fluid. She flows from her veins and her breasts. She is sanguine and lacteal, red and white. But her sanguinity whitens. She, Irigaray writes, "will from now on become associated with nourishing and fluidifying *lymph*, nearly *white* while she loses her blood."[11] She bleeds out, nourishing him.

The maternalfeminine is not, for the paternalmasculine, a robust other. She is always, Irigaray writes, "just the mother again [*plutôt encore de la mère*]," signifying "a return to the mother's milk, to the generosity of her blood."[12] She remains mother, and not other.

Antigone flows differently. Her blood flows differently. It overflows kinship, and nature-culture with it.

Antigone is not a mother.[13] Her name, *anti-gonē*, means "anti-generation," "anti-production," "anti-offspring," "anti-birth." This translation renders Antigone *anti*. It renders her negatively:

defining her by what she is not, and doing so on someone else's terms, according to someone else's values. On hommohumanism's terms, Antigone is only what she is not. She is only opposing.

But *anti* can signify *counter*. *Counter* can mean *counter*-productive. It can mean differently productive: productive of difference(s).

This other translation renders Antigone as "counter-generation," "counter-production," "counter-birth."[14] It renders her positively, as *other*. She can become *pro*—but *pro altero*: *pro* something else, something other, on her terms, according to her values. Antigone's *pro*—her *anti* as *counter*—performs a double movement. She opposes and proposes. *Counter* proposes an alternative. It proposes something other, something different. It is de-constructive: critical and creative, concurrently.

Antigone is not a mother. She is an other. She is not an "other of the same." She is an *other* other. She resists a systematic, sublimating consignment to nourishing hommosexuality. Her sexual difference flows differently. She is differently feminine.

Antigone does not animate or embody the maternalfeminine. She resists a collapse of femininity into maternity. She animates a different sexual difference. She proposes a counter-femininity. She embodies an other sexuality, an other femininity. She embodies the filial-feminine (with a hyphen, for spacing).

This hyphen inscribes what Irigaray, recasting Hegel, calls the negative. The negative marks limits and the recognition and acceptance of them. It makes, or leaves, space for an other. It can enable access to an other, within or across sexual difference(s). But this access depends on accepting limits and recognizing this other's irreducible otherness. The negative opens and keeps open a space *between*, and a possibility for inter-active relation. It makes, or leaves, space for otherness, and for love.

The negative traces the difference that sexual difference(s) delineates. It traces the limit that preserves difference—and sexual difference(s) first of all. Sexual difference(s) is the fluid through which other differences flow, such as nature and culture. Nature-culture is sexuate. It is a matter of sexual difference(s) (rather than the other way around).

So is subjectivity. Subjects cannot surmount the negative of sexual difference(s). The sexual limits that the negative traces trace subjective limits. As Irigaray writes, "'I am sexed' implies 'I am not everything' ['*je suis sexué(e)*' *implique* '*je ne suis pas tout(e)*']."[15] That "I am not everything" enables difference, otherness, others, contact, even exchange. These can occur in a space *between*, such as a hyphen-vein, through which sexual difference(s) flows.

Hommohumanism controls these flows. It flows freely through this hyphen-vein. But it either prevents "woman" from flowing through (as Hegel does) or allows her to flow through only maternally—only in a flood of nurturing blood and milk.

Antigone flows differently. Her flow is filial-feminine. Its hyphen marks limits on both: relational and sexual differences. It keeps one from collapsing into the other. Antigone is a sister, and a woman. She is irreducibly both. The former depends on the latter, but remains irreducible to it. (Because "filial" can accommodate sexual difference[s], there could be a filial-masculine.) Neither can dissolve (into) the other.

Were such dissolution possible, Antigone would resist it. She does not wish to mimic hommosexuality's dissolution of the feminine into the maternalfeminine. She does not seek to replace one femininity with another. She seeks to engender an other femininity, a different femininity. Antigone is not anti-maternal.[16] She is pro-filial. The two sexualities are not mutually exclusive. Femininity has room for both.

So might Antigone. She might conceivably be counter-maternal and pro-filial. She might offer a different maternity, one that produces something other than a child. Perhaps her counter-maternity propagates her filial-femininity?

Not a mother, Antigone is a sister. She is even, Jacques Derrida writes, an "eternal sister," one who "fixes, seizes, transits, transfigures herself in this character."[17] She is solely sororal, and solely sanguine. Her blood flows differently because of a different sexual difference, an other femininity.[18]

Antigone does not lose her blood. She does not liquefy into lymph. She resists such a transferential transfusion (*trans*fusion and trans*fusion*). She remains vibrantly red-blooded.

Antigone remains bloody. She remains only blood-y, never milk-y. She is not doubly fluid. She is a one-fluid woman. She is singularly sanguine. (Her menstrual blood regularly reiterates her nonmaternity.)

Antigone's different flow, her different sexual difference, is disruptive. It disrupts natural-cultural feminine fluid economies. Their "mechanics of fluids" are maternalfeminine, and so double: sanguine and lacteal.

Antigone's filial-feminine flow is sanguine and sisterly. Her kinship ties are to her siblings—to all her siblings.[19]

Antigone's different flows make fluid difference(s). In her bloody differences flow her different sexual differences, her different kinship relations: as counter-maternal and filial-feminine. Antigone writes her counter-maternity, which means different ways of doing kinship and sexual differences, with her blood. Her blood, her fluidity, her maternity, and her humanity are written, and rewritten, together. (So a reference to one refers, implicitly, to them all.) Through these bloody differences flows a different humanity.

Kinship ties bind Antigone to filial duties, to familial and pious obligations, such as burying her dead brother's body. Leaving these duties undone would pain her—more than death. As she tells Kreon, "if I had endured the son / of my own mother to lie dead without a grave, / *that* would have brought me grief."[20] She names her brother by relation (as brother, "the son of my own mother"), not by name (Polyneikes). Her words appraise kinship relations over nominal identities.

They also appraise filial bonds over maternal (or matrimonial) bonds. Standing before her tomb, Antigone announces that she would perform this action (of burying Polyneikes's corpse), take this risk, incur this punishment, only for filial bonds. Her stated reason is her brother's singular irreplaceability. As she explains, "My husband dead, I could have had another, and / a child from someone else, if I had lost the first; / but with my mother and my father both concealed / in Hades, no more brothers ever could be born. / By such a law as this I honored you, my own / dear brother, higher than them all."[21]

These last words are telling. They reveal her valuative priorities: filial bonds over maternal ones. Her filial-femininity entails a different valuation from the established, "natural-cultural" primacy of maternity over sorority. Such primacy coincides with, or follows from, a hommohumanistic decrease of feminine into maternalfeminine.

Antigone's different flow threatens to disrupt sexual differences—doubly.

1. Appraising kinship relations over nominal identities (appraising relation, and hence plurality, over individuality) also appraises filial bonds over maternal (or matrimonial) bonds.[22] Standing before her tomb, Antigone announces that she would perform this action (of burying Polyneikes's corpse), take this risk, incur this punishment, only for filial bonds. She honors her siblings singularly. She would risk burying only a dead sibling, not a dead husband or a dead child.

Antigone's filial-feminine values diverge from the established, natural-cultural primacy of maternity over sorority. In doing so, they resist hommohumanism's channeling of the feminine into the maternalfeminine through the paternalmasculine. They disrupt established sexual differences by redirecting feminine flow.

2. Antigone's different flow also threatens to disrupt specific sexual differences. Her different femininity imperils Kreon's masculinity. Her filial actions threaten to emasculate him. In doing so, her fil-

ial-femininity threatens to disrupt political order. It threatens to enact a sexual switch. Kreon recognizes this possibility: "it's clear enough that I'm no man, but she's the man, / if she can get away with holding power like this."[23] She, and not he, would be a man. She, and not he, might then be king.

To threaten Kreon's hommosexuality threatens his political power, and vice versa. For him, a sexual threat is a political threat, and a political threat is a sexual threat. In his hommosexual *polis*, sexuality and power are enmeshed, exclusively. They are for men only. Others are not included.

Kreon cannot abide this potent threat. At stake are his masculinity and his hommosexual political rule, bound together. These are his priorities. For him, political power trumps family values. Blood-bonds mean less to him than civic ties.[24]

Antigone cares about kinship. Kreon cares about kingship.

So, he declares, "whether she's my sister's child, or tied to me / closer by blood than all my household under Zeus, / she won't escape from a most evil doom."[25] Her "most evil doom" will be living burial.

Burying Antigone alive executes two blood-related objectives.

1. It quells her different sexual difference and its sisterly, sanguine flow. Her filial-femininity has real political potency. It threatens to undo the existing community, over which Kreon rules. Through Antigone's fluid difference, Irigaray writes, "forces rise up and threaten to devastate the community. To turn it upside down [*De la mettre sens dessus dessous*]. Refusing to be that unconscious nourishing ground of nature"—or culture.[26] Refusing a naturalized dissolution of "feminine" into "maternal."

2. It quells her filial-femininity, her sororal sanguinity, without creating an other communal threat. The preset penalty for burying Polyneikes's corpse is ston-

ing.²⁷ But Antigone, who buries it twice, is Kreon's kin. To have a blood-relative stoned would bring *miasma*, a blood-pollution. This blood-pollution would spill into and saturate the city. To avoid this contamination and its effects, Kreon opts instead to inter Antigone in a man-made cave, leaving her a little food. This way, her death will be "natural." A "natural" death would not flood Thebes in *miasma*. It would not cause a bloody problem.

But Antigone causes one nonetheless. She has already imbalanced blood. As a child of incest, her blood comes contaminated. It has already confounded nature-culture and its founding, sanguine prohibition of incest. It already flows differently, inhumanly.

It also flows differently, sexually. Her sanguine sexual difference rethreatens nature-culture, which has tried to contain her incestuous blood. But nature-culture might not be able to contain her sexually different, or differently sexual, flow. It might not be able to repress her singular fluidity, her sororal sanguinity, which redirects femininity's flows (in the plural). Her filial-feminine flow threatens hommohumanistic nature-culture with a tidal wave—of blood.

With Antigone, Irigaray writes, "the balance of blood has been undone, has been altered and dissolved [*s'est défait, s'est altéré et dissolu*]."²⁸ Or, through Antigone, the balance of blood has undone itself, has altered and dissolved itself. This bloody undoing, whether by or through Antigone, overflows nature-culture. Her sanguine sexual difference can flood nature-culture, and hommohumanism with it.

Antigone is all about blood. Blood embodies and enlivens Antigone. Her living depends on blood, on its corporeal circulation. Blood is a bodily postal system. In bodies of living vertebrates, it delivers oxygen and nutrients to cells and delivers waste from cells. Antigone, as a living animal, lives on blood. Blood capacitates biological survival.

Life, too, lives on blood. When blood no longer flows in a body, that body no longer lives. Antigone's death, like her life, is a matter of blood. Interred alive, she hangs herself in her tomb, using a piece of cloth (probably her veil).[29] Her death likely comes due to occluded blood vessels (such as her carotid artery or her jugular vein). Her life ends when her blood stops flowing.

Her bloodflow's stoppage leads to bloodshed. Antigone's death starts a suicidal chain reaction: of Haimon, who falls on his sword, spurting blood onto Antigone's corpse; and then of Eurydike, who dies from self-inflicted blows after learning of Haimon's death.

Antigone is all about blood. So is *Antigone*, the Sophoklean drama through which blood courses, spilling onto almost every character and conflict. *Antigone* nearly overflows with blood: from Polyneikes's and Eteokles's deaths, from filial bonds, from the blood-soaked dust Antigone uses to bury Polyneikes's body (twice), from Haimon's and Eurydike's deaths, from Antigone's singularly sanguine fluidity.

Blood flows over boundaries of nature-culture. It threatens to overflow them, flood them. Nature-culture responds to protect its hommohumanistic heritage and privileged position. Kreon, acting and expositing on its behalf, contains the threat of Antigone. Nature-culture inters her, twice. Before entombing her, it inters her in a dehumanization. It renders her an *other* other: other than human. It recasts Antigone as an other animal.

Kreon's guard reports this recasting. He recounts Antigone's discovery of Polyneikes's unburied corpse (after she had buried it). Following a windstorm, the guard sees "this girl here wailing bitterly aloud, / in the piercing voice of a mother bird who sees her nest / is empty and her bed bereft of baby chicks."[30] His account displaces Antigone. She becomes a bird.

She becomes, specifically, a mother bird. The guard's account doubly displaces Antigone. It alters her animality, from human to bird. It also alters her kinship position, from sister to mother.

This second displacement effects a third. Because Antigone's femininity and her kinship position flow together, as filial-feminine, altering one alters the other. For Antigone, a different kinship position means a different femininity.

By staging these displacements, the guard reiterates that species, sexuality, and kinship flow together for Antigone. To name one invokes all three.

The guard does so in the voice of hommohumanism. By articulating these displacements, the guard gives voice to hommohumanism. His account recalls its netting together of women and birds (and other animals). It reiterates women's natural position: culturally subsumed, as maternalfeminine. The guard, it seems, attempts to recapture Antigone—this time, for Kreon, the embodiment of hommohumanism. He does capture her and bring her before Kreon. The guard's capture of Antigone, alive, in hommohumanism heralds Kreon's burial of her, alive, in a man-made cave.

(The guard names Antigone as a bird. He does not name Antigone as a fish. Might he have? Birds and fish—and beasts and women—are captured together, in the same hommohumanistic nets. In its Ode to Man, *Antigone*'s chorus names birds and fish together. So, in a different register, does Luce Irigaray: "fish, bird, of course!"[31] Her invocation comes via her renaming women as divine. Fish, moreover, move through fluids. They, like Antigone, navigate flows. Perhaps an other revival of Antigone might recast her as a fish.)

Antigone becomes a mother bird by passing into hommohumanism's anthropological machine. It seems geared to do two things: to animalize the human and to humanize the animal. These two operations seem to perform two displacements. They seem to displace: to move human and nonhuman to other places, other positions. They seem to displace the human to an animal "outside" and displace the animal to a human "inside."

This seemingly double displacement discloses a state of exception. A state of exception, Giorgio Agamben writes, is "a zone of indeterminacy in which the outside is nothing but the exclusion of an inside and the inside is in turn only the inclusion of an outside."[32] A state of exception is empty. It is called "the open," because it remains open, vacant. It marks a caesura. A state of exception exposes a passage in which no passage occurs.

Human and nonhuman do not pass one another in this passage. The anthropological machine displaces them to "outside" and "inside" *of the human*. "Outside" and "inside" are relative to the human, who remains the measure. "Outside" and "inside" do not move human and nonhuman to *other* positions. Human and nonhuman shift to other-within-the-same positions. Nonhuman becomes an "other of the same."

These seemingly different operations are two movements within one operation. This anthropological machine is an anthropologizing machine. It humanizes and dehumanizes: humanizing the nonhuman animal and dehumanizing the human animal. Humanizing and dehumanizing are reciprocal, dialectical. One coincides with the other. As Agamben writes, "the total humanization of the [nonhuman] animal coincides with a total animalization of man."[33]

The anthropological machine is an anthropologizing machine. It effects anthropogenesis (and deanthropogenesis). Anthropogenesis, Agamben writes, "is what results from the caesura and articulation between human and [nonhuman] animal."[34] From this caesura, this open *between*, comes *anthrōpos*, the human. (*Anthrōpos*, the human, quickly becomes *anēr*, the hu*man*. The anthropologizing machine is hommohumanistic.)

The anthropological machine humanizes and dehumanizes according to its account of "human." It humanizes and dehumanizes according to what, or whom, it "counts" as human. Its "human" accounting is humanistic, and hommosexual. Men and women count differently. They count in proportion to a hommohumanistic account of "human." The paternalmasculine counts fully. The maternalfeminine counts less, but still counts. She, like he, still counts as human—though not as hu*man*. They, this couple, are still humanized.

Antigone's filial-feminine sexuality counts otherwise. So it does not count hommohumanistically. The anthropological machine does not count it. (It cannot: it is not calibrated to do so.) This other sexuality does not count as human. The anthropologizing machine dis-counts this—her—other sexuality. This discounting is dehumanizing.

The anthropological machine humanizes and dehumanizes. It does not animalize.

Antigone's anthropological displacement does not animalize her. She is already an animal: a feminine human animal. Displaced, she becomes a feminine nonhuman animal. Her difference, her otherness, compounds. She becomes a different other, an *other* other, one who does not count, or no longer counts, as human. Antigone becomes an other animal. She becomes a different animal.

There are different animals. There is no "the animal." "The animal" does not exist.

"The animal" is a humanistic name. As "nature" is cultural, so "animal" is human. "The animal" is a humanistic shorthand for "nonhuman." It is a reductive, hommohumanistic name for what (and not who) the anthropological machine does not count as human.

"The animal" is a hommohumanistic designation: a *de*-signation, a discounting. It is *a* designation, a single name, for what (and not who) hommohumanism tames, manipulates, masters, dominates. "The animal," Derrida writes, "is a word that *men* have instituted, a name they have given themselves the right to give to the living other [*à l'autre vivant*]"³⁵ (my emphasis). "The animal" is one of hommohumanism's nicknames for "other."

There is no "the animal" because there is no "the other." There is only *an* other. There are only others. Each other is different. Each other is, and makes, a difference.

"Other" is already plural in the singular. So is "animal." They work like "difference(s)." For other and animal, the singular is already in the plural. There is, Derrida writes, "no Animal in the general singular [*il n'y a pas l'Animal au singulier général*], separated from human by a single indivisible limit," which is why "I would like to have the plural of animals heard in the singular."³⁶

Animal becomes animal(s). (I would like to have a corollary for Antigone: having the plural heard in the singular.)

Antigone is an animal(s).

Antigone passes into, but not through, the hommohumanistic anthropological machine. She gets jammed in this machine. She has jammed this machine. (It is as if this machine were made for handling only solids, and Antigone is fluid.)

She is *inter*. She lives *inter animala*: between animal(s), between animalities. She moves *inter animala*: in the passage, between identities. She is a human-bird. More graphically precisely, she is a human-animal-bird-animal, or (human-animal)-(bird-animal). She flows through this passage.

By doing so, Antigone flows through an other, double passage, between identities. By living between animalities, she lives between kinship positions, and between femininities. She is, more graphically, a (filial-feminine-human-animal)-(maternal-feminine-bird-animal).

The anthropological machine exposes an empty interstice, a caesura, between human and animal. It exposes it: *ecce apertum*. It goes no further.

Antigone goes further. She enters. She *inter*-s. She moves between. She works the interval.

Antigone *inter*-s and moves in this interstice, this passage (perhaps a vein?), which is no longer empty. Her movement *between* exposes the porosity of these humanistic names: human, animal, natural, cultural. She exposes humanism and its erected barriers to be porous. Humanism is holey. Air or liquid can pass. Antigone, fluid and feminine, passes.

Antigone loosen(d)s "human." She undoes its edges, unties its moorings. She unbinds "human" from "humanism." She unhinges hommohumanism's insistence that "human" can be only one way, that there can be only one "human."

Antigone is antihommohumanistic. She might be inhuman, nonhuman, dehuman, subhuman, posthuman, or some other "human." She is not antihuman. She is pro-human. She is for an other human, an other humanity.

Antigone animates an other humanity. She does so by flowing differently, by overflowing hommohumanistic, natural-cultural kinship. Antigone does kinship differently. She, Judith Butler writes, "upsets the vocabulary of kinship that is a precondition of the human," so that "if kinship is a precondition of the human, then Antigone is the occasion for a new field of the human."[37]

Antigone animates an other humanity. She does so by becoming an animal(s), by flowing differently through human-animal relations. Antigone lives human-animal differently.[38]

Antigone revives humanity, differently. She revives an other humanity. She generates a counter-humanity. She does so as an animal(s).

This counter-humanity that Antigone induces is a human-animality. Antigone is a human-animal.

"Human-animal" discloses the inseparability of human and animal. Its hyphen graphically insists on this inseparability. In doing so, it reiterates that a human is an animal. "Human" *is* "animal," an animal, a part of "animal." Animal is bigger than human.

Human-animal recognizes this difference. It does not try, as humanism does, to subsume animality into humanity. Such a subsuming would fashion human as animal-plus: animal plus rationality, animal plus culture, animal plus technology, and so forth. Human would become bigger than animal. It would be able to corral and contain animality.

But human cannot subsume, swallow, co-opt, digest animal. Animal is bigger than human. Human-animal accepts this difference. It perceives its humanity as part of its animality. It accepts its humanity as its kind of animality, its way of being animal—different from other kinds and other ways.

Human cannot subsume animal. Nor can human oppose animal, analytically or aggressively. Human and nonhuman could be opposed, compared, as related terms. Human and animal could not.

Human-animal does not eliminate an opposition of human and animal, because they are not opposed. Their "opposition" would come from humanism's division of them, as human/animal. Calling to end this "opposition" would accept humanism's terms. Suggesting that, Matthew Calarco writes, "the human-animal distinction can no longer and ought no longer to be maintained" would play into humanism's hands.[39] It would accept a humanistic distinction of human and animal. It would accept a humanistic synonymy of nonhuman and animal. It would also accept a humanistic indistinction of "animal" as singular, as if "the animal" exists.

These acceptions would misplace difference(s). They would risk eliminating difference(s) that exist between human and animal. They would risk recalibrating, rather than jamming, the anthropological machine. This recalibration would be for species rather than sexuality. But the machinery would remain intact, and operational.

Human-animal neither humanizes "animal" nor animalizes "human." It neither humanizes nor dehumanizes. Both are humanistic operations. Human-animal does something different. It dehumanisticizes human. It dislodges human from humanism. It dismantles, deconstructs, the anthropological machine.

Antigone is the first posthumanist. She interrupts hommohumanism before it is initially articulated. She appears on stage before the chorus's Ode to Man. She disturbs it, disrupts it, dislodges it, supplements it, from before its beginning.

She disturbs, disrupts, dislodges, supplements what has not yet come. She does not wait to respond to hommohumanism and its Ode to Man, which engenders "humanity." She presponds. She is already posthumanist, before hommohumanism's self-delivery. (She is, already, temporally out of joint.)

Antigone is the first posthumanist by being the first human-animal, the first to engender this other humanity. She can do so only in relation, in (p)response, to humanity's initial articulation.

Antigone is the first posthumanist. She might not be the first posthuman.

I have written that she is the first posthuman.[40] Now, I am not so sure.

I cast Antigone as the first posthuman based on humanism's sense of "human," of what counts as human. I accepted humanism's terms. Those terms are binary: human and inhuman (which is also subhuman)—one or the other. Antigone is antihumanist. She is posthumanist. On humanism's terms, she becomes inhuman, anti-human, antihu*man*. On hommohumanism's terms, she is the first posthuman.

But those terms are not the only ones. They are no longer ones I accept. I still think that Antigone exceeds humanism, flooding it, overflowing its borders. But I think she can do so without having to yield "human" to humanism.

Antigone need not cede "human." She can revive it. She can revive a different "human," a different humanity. She can induce a counter-humanity. This counter-humanity would be a human-animality. It would be a humanity that embraces (its) animality.

There can be more than one humanity. The humanity produced by the anthropological machine need not be the only one. Human need not be hommohumanistic. There can be other humanities, different humanities, plural humanities.

These other humanities offer other ways to supplement humanism and its "human." One way is by moving past "human," becoming posthuman. An other way is by moving through "human," supplementing it by flowing through and overflowing it.

Antigone moves through human and animal. She flows through the hyphen-vein that grafts, but spaces, them.

Human and animal are inseparable. They are not collapsible. They are bound, but different. They are bound and bounded. But their limits are not fixed. They are movable, and they move. They remain unsettled.

They remain so because, Jean-Christophe Bailly writes, "animals have never been able to stay in place, neither by themselves nor in the thought and dreams of humans. *The animals*, this border-boundary [*cette limite-frontière*] between the human and the beast, have—without effort, freely—never ceased to render this border-boundary an unsettled one."[41] Animals, of many kinds, unsettle boundaries. They disturb borders. (Antigone is one such animal.)

These border-boundaries remain unsettled, particularly at points of contact. But they remain. These border-boundaries become loosen(d)ed. But they endure, and live on.

Human-animal marks both: bond and difference(s). Through this hyphen, "human" and "animal" come into contact. They come, Bailly writes, into "close contact [*côtoiement*], always singular and always made of touches, that is the ordinary mode of the bond [*lien*] between them," one "barely bound [*à peine lié*], always happening [*survenant*]."[42] They contact. They come into contact. They touch. But their contact is loose, and still coming.

Antigone is an animal(s). Her human-animality is not exclusive. She is human and nonhuman: human and avian, a human and a bird. She lives *between*.

She realizes human-animality and avian-animality. She becomes an other animal: a bird. She becomes an other animal(s).

Antigone's animality is plural. Plurality requires differences, which require limits. Plurality requires the negative, as a recognition of limits and limitations. Human and bird are discrete. They have edges. Their edges touch in Antigone. Antigone even loosen(d)s their edges.

But she does not erase them. Antigone recognizes and respects limits. Limits are what let her live *between*. Without limits, there can be no *between*. Without limits, there can be no differences. Without differences, there can be no relations—no room, no space, for movement, or even breathing.

These limits are not absolutely fixed. They are movable. They move. They remain unsettled, undone.

Antigone engenders an other sexuality. She engenders an other humanity. These engenderings are entwined.

Antigone is *inter animala*. She might be interspecies. She might be dehumanized or differently humanized. But she is not desexualized. She remains resolutely feminine.

She is a feminine animal(s). Her feminine sexuality endures any zoological displacement. She passes between human-animality and avian-animality through sexual difference(s). Animal ontology, like nature-culture, flows through sexual difference(s). Sexual difference is preontological. Any existence, even existence as such, arrives via sexual difference(s). "We cannot do," Irigaray writes, "without the horizon of sexual difference. No world is produced or reproduced without sexual difference. Plants, animals, gods, elements of the universe, all are sexed [*sexué*]."[43] Sexual difference(s) is what is.

Animal existence is sexuate from the start, and sexed all the way down. To be an animal is to be sexed and sexuate. Human or nonhuman, Antigone is a feminine animal—in that order. Living denominations, such as "human" and "bird," are always already sexuate.

Antigone, an animal of whatever sort, remains feminine. She is a feminine animal. She is a feminanimal. Antigone's feminanimality graphically enfolds her sexuality and her animality (of whatever kind). I graphically bleed sexuality and animality together because they bleed together. Neither can live without the other.

Feminanimality denotes that difference(s) is always plural. It denotes that sexual differences and animal differences crossflow. They interflow. They flow through one another. They cannot be separated.

These flows precede any flows into species channels. A feminanimal's sexuality is more vital than her humanity. Her sexuality and her living are vitally interwoven. They flow together.

These differential interflows of sexuality and animality make methodological differences. Feminanimality flows animal studies through sexual studies. If animality, of whatever sort, is sexed and sexuate, then thinking through animality means thinking animality through sexual difference(s). Sexual differences are animal differences. Sexual differences make differences animally. Animal studies should account for these differences. This accounting remains undone.

Flowing animal studies through sexual difference(s) opens methodological channels. Animal studies and sexual studies address themselves to hommohumanism. They seek to disturb hommohumanism by bringing differences to bear on it. They bring different differences, but they have similar desires and tactics. Flowing animal studies through sexual studies compounds their differential potency.

Through these crossflows, animal studies and sexual studies can become mutual resources. For example, Irigaray's writings on sexual difference(s) can contribute significantly to animal studies. Animal studies can, correlatively, upset any latent humanism remaining in sexuality studies. They can co-respond to one another, as different ways of conceiving and realizing difference(s).

These co-respondences of animal studies and sexuality studies bear on conceptions of life, of living. Living is a matter of sexual and animal differences, so sexual and animal differences matter for life. Antigone's feminanimality activates a rethinking of life, of relation—of her relation to life. Antigone is for life. She is *pro vitas*. She fights for life. She values living, maybe even supremely.

But being for life does not quarantine life from death, the living from the dead. Life and death are different. They are differences. They are not oppositions. The living and the dead are not opposed. Life and death, the living and the dead, are on the same side. They are on the side of life. There is no other side. Life and death, life-and-death, life-death: they live together, on the side of life. They are for life.[44]

Antigone is for life. She is for life *and* for the dead. She is for living with the dead. The dead live on with her.

She is for life, but not for "life itself." For her, for life, there is no such thing.

Feminanimality's sexual and animal flows recall blood flows through, across, over kinship. Antigone confuses kinship, confounding its hommohumanistic flows. Her filial-femininity undoes kinship's sedimented structures. It conceives of an other way of kinship.

So does her feminanimality. Feminanimality transfuses kinship. It generates an other kinship, a counter-kinship. This counter-kinship is based on blood—but on blood-flow rather than blood-lines, on lifeblood rather than lineage. Feminanimality induces, or discloses, a vital kinship of living.

This kinship induces relations with differences. It does not delete differences. It does not erase limits. It respects them—and relates them, bringing them into contact. Living is coming, and coming into contact: with others, with differences, with limits.

These limits can be corporeal, sexual, zoological, material, mortal, ethical, ontological. Living lives at these limits. There, it opens ontologically, to what it might be. Living at the limits realizes being. The limits are places of proximity, contact. Perhaps only at the limits, Bailly writes, "only in proximity to animals, then, do we truly encounter the whole and fabulous conjugation of the verb *to be*."[45] Being lives at the limits.

These living limits, these contact relations, are, Derrida writes, "at once intimate and abyssal, and they are never totally objectified."[46] They are never final. They are coming: done and undone. They are almost respiring.

These living limits, these coming-into-contacts, are porous. Living is porous. It is a porosity.

Porosity respects differences while allowing exchange between them. Porosity lets limits breathe. It lets them breathe together. It lets them inspire and expire, with others. Inspiration and expiration name ways of passing. They name ways of passing between: between others, between animalities, between birth and death, between the living and the dead.

Breathing is passing. It is a passage *between*. It is a living passage, between birth and death. Breathe, and blood flows. Living continues. Stop breathing, and blood stops flowing. Living does not continue. Breath and blood flow circulate, between inspiration and expiration, which interdepend.

Living is porous. Breath flows through it. Living respires. Living is respiring. It is, Bailly writes, "as if respiration condensed rhythmically the dramatic tension of the existence of the living," in "this coming and going through which the outside and the inside communicate."[47]

Living is porous, and porosity is plural.[48] There are other porosities, and other passages, with others. Through porosity, living relates, responds, respires.

The living names those who respire, who breathe. The living names those who share air.

Animals respire. Plants respire. They breathe air in and out of their bodies—their porous bodies, their bodily porosities. They breathe differently, in different ways, at different rates. They breathe together, as (among) the living. They breathe, with others. They respire—inspire and expire—and living transpires (*trans*pires).

Living, breathing, are matters of being and relation (of ontology and ethics). They are matters of being in relation. Living is living with. Living means living with others, and other others. Living means living with and through differences.

These others include those no longer living. The living are more than the living. Living is living with the dead. The living includes the dead.

This mortal inclusion does not "mortalize" living's orientation. It does not aim the living toward the dead, or life toward death. It does not reduce *zōē* or *bios* to *thanatos*. It does not cryptify, or en-crypt, living. It accepts that the living are related to the dead: materially, affectively, memorially, morally, mortally. It recognizes that the living pass into the dead. It realizes that mortality means porosity, and porosity entails vulnerability.

Living vulnerability is mutual. Vulnerability comes *between* the living. It comes as a double mutual vulnerability. The living are doubly, mutually, vulnerable: to others and to death.

Living comes through vulnerability, being vulnerable *to*. Being vulnerable *to* calls for being responsive *to*. Vulnerability leads to living as response-ability. It leads the living to conceive, Calarco writes, of "life as responsivity, where life is understood not exclusively but broadly and inclusively," and porously.[49] Vulnerability recalls that living is porous, respiring, relational, coming.

Living comes, Bailly writes, "in the fact that something arrives (rather than nothing), the fact that this arrival or this coming continues," as living "advances, arranges, spreads out, redistributes, borders, invades, and overruns itself. As the living, we are enveloped in living, in its divergences, its impulses, its folds [*dans ses écarts, ses élans, ses replis*]."⁵⁰

Living comes with others. Living comes, with others. Living happens in the plural.

Living means living with. It means living in relation, with others. Living means relating, inter-acting, morally and politically.

Antigone lives relations. She lives with and through relations, with living and dead others. Her living relations are *poly*: political, animal, moral, mortal. They engender a polyzoontopolitics. This neologism enfolds *poly* (plural), *zōē* (living), *zōon* (animal), and ontic (being). It enfolds them as a way of political(ly) living.

It enfolds them, through Antigone, as an other way of approaching, or doing, biopolitics. Biopolitics is a politics of sovereignty, of life and death. Its life is divided, between *zōē* and *bios*. (Loosely translated, *zōē* and *bios* name "fact of living" and "way of living.")

This division is hierarchical and humanistic. It reiterates divisions between nature and culture, between nonhuman and human. Nature and nonhuman share in *zōē*. Only culture and human inhabit *zōē* and *bios*. Biopolitics reveals itself as *bios*-politics: a human politics. It reveals itself as humanistic, exclusive and excluding.

Biopolitics becomes a politics of sacrifice. It sacrifices *others*. It decides others' deaths. It sovereignly puts to death or lets die. These others' deaths are means to an end: biopolitics' survival. *Bios* lives on *thanatos*. Biopolitics recalibrates the anthropological machine, turning it into the anthropological death machine, in the service of sovereignty.

Biopolitics does not grieve these deaths, these lives lost. These lives, these deaths, remain ungrievable—like Polyneikes's. Kreon denies Polyneikes grievability by dehumanizing him. (He does so after Polyneikes's death, showing the porosity of the living and the dead.) Kreon dis-counts Polyneikes as human. Polyneikes's unburied corpse becomes animal food, a "treasure sweet / for watching birds to feed on at their pleasure."⁵¹

Biopolitics re-recalibrates the anthropological machine, now turning it into a calculator. The anthropological machine counts. It counts who counts: who counts as human, as *bios*, as a who. It decides, Butler writes, "what counts as a livable life and a grievable death"; it determines "whose lives can be marked as lives, and whose deaths will count as deaths."[52] It dis-counts those that do not count, or count as other. Their lives it sacrifices, for the sake of its survival. Biopolitics becomes a politics of death for life.

(Nazism exemplifies a biopolitical anthropological machine. The Nazi machine decides who counts and excludes all others: racial others, ethnic others, sexual others, medical others, psychological others. These other lives do not count as human lives. These lives are subhuman. Their deaths do not count as grievable deaths. Their deaths feed the Nazi machine, which can preserve those lives that count only by killing, or letting die, those that do not. The Nazi machine normalizes, *normalizes*, these killings. They become law—as does Kreon's edict, declaring Polyneikes nonmournable. These parallels pose a question: might Kreon be a Nazi *avant la lettre*?)[53]

Biopolitics' anthropological machine dis-counts Antigone twice. As a feminanimal, she is doubly other(ed). Kreon's biopolitical machine sacrifice her, to save its sovereignty from threat and its sovereign territory from *miasma*. It sacrifices Antigone by burying her alive, leaving her to die, "naturally."

Antigone again jams the machine. Her suicide evades sacrifice. Her death denies biopolitics its desired sacrifice, its sacrificial desire. Her death sacrifices biopolitical sacrifice. It denies biopolitics the ability to decide life and death. Antigone, not Kreon, decides her death. Based on her decision, Haimon and Eurydike decide on death. These deaths bleed on biopolitics. Biopolitics drowns in their blood.

Biopolitics cannot survive as *bio*politics. Its survival depends on its undoing. This undoing might expose *bios*, no longer immunizing it against others. It might pluralize and democratize *bios* across *zōē*. It might reorient *bios* to birth. Biopolitics might survive, but as undone. It might survive, but not as biopolitics.

Perhaps it might survive as polyzoontopolitics. It might live on as a politics of the living, in its plurality and porosity. It might live on as a politics of *zōē* and *zōon*, of living animals. A polyzoontopolitics would be a politics of the living. It would be a politics of exposure: of the living to the living and the nonliving. It would count the living and the dead, life and death.

A polyzoontopolitics would be, or do, biopolitics otherwise. It would be a biopolitics for which, Cary Wolfe writes, "the biopolitical point is a newly expanded community of the living."[54] The point is a new way of living with, living together. The point is an other kinship, an other way of relating, among the living. This vital counter-kinship of the living is material, mortal, ethical, ontological. It would be a polyzoontovital kinship: of breath and blood, plurality and porosity.

A vital counter-kinship of the living is not vitalist. The living names a plurality, not a multitude. It names a plurality of living animals (and nonanimals). It enfolds the dead in relation to the living. It does not name a vital force, a pulse of life. It names a community of those who have (or have had) pulses.

Antigone's pulse flows through, between, over borders. It flows through her filial-feminine sexuality, across her feminanimality, between her human-animality, over natural-cultural hommohumanistic bindings that try to corral, constrain, restrain, repress, suppress, submerge, subsume her. Antigone flows on. She, like other animals, seems never willing, or able, to stay in her place.

Her species does not stay in place. Her feminanimality moves between human and avian. Kreon's guard renders her an other animal: a bird. More specifically, he renders her a mother bird. Her feminanimality shifts, between filial-human and maternal-avian. She can be maternal only inhumanly. Her reproductive possibilities are still counter-human.

These feminanimal shifts do not involve fluid shifts. They do not affect Antigone's fluid, which remains singularly sanguine. Mother birds are milkless. Unlike mammalian mothers, they do not produce milk to feed their offspring. Whether human or bird (or both or between), whether filial or maternal, Antigone is only blood-y, never milk-y.

Recast as a mother bird, Antigone is nonhuman, but not necessarily subhuman. Birds, for example, live thought. Birds, Bailly writes, "do not have this movement of thought, they embody it; they *are* this thought."⁵⁵ Birds are thinking. Birds move thought.

They move it beyond human-animals. They lead the way, and human-animals follow. Birds bring messages. They bear signs. Human-animals follow birds into the future.

Birds play special roles. They play special roles in Sophokles's *Antigone*. No other animal receives more than a mention. But birds appear in four scenes, playing four roles.

1. Birds play captives. They are among those captured by man in hommohumanistic nets (along with women, beasts, and fish).

2. Birds play mothers. Or a bird plays a mother. Kreon's guard renames Antigone as a screaming mother bird. In doing so, he displaces Antigone's animality, sexuality, and kinship position.

3. Birds play scavengers. They prey on Polyneikes's dead body. They feed on his corpse.

4. Birds play prophets. They are vital for augury, a practice of foretelling the future by reading bird behaviors.

An augur is a seer: of signs, of the future. An augur attends to nonhumans, particularly birds. Birds deliver messages between divinity and humanity. An augur watches for divine messages by watching the behaviors of birds. An augur is a religious figure, a diviner, who decrypts messages from gods to humans borne by birds. Birds become prophetic signs that an augur reads and interprets. Through augury, birds signify and divine the future.

Kreon consults an augur, Teiresias, a blind prophet who sees signs. Teiresias arrives onstage immediately following Antigone's interment. His message is that he has no message. When he performs his augury, he perceives chaos. He hears "the birds give unknown voice, screeching / in evil frenzy, babbling incoherently."[56] The birds offer no signs, except of frenzy. Their wings whir. They tear bloodily at one another. They screech in unknown voices that do not signify.

Their screeches recall Antigone's avian cry, wailing over an empty nest. They also recall Polyneikes's avian cry, "a piercing / scream like an eagle."[57] His cry precedes hers—and like hers, his is reported: by the chorus, in its entrance song. His cry comes as he approaches Thebes to battle his brother, Eteokles, for political control. In battle, the brothers slay one another. Polyneikes's corpse is left unburied, setting the stage for *Antigone*'s action.

Polyneikes's avian cry precedes, and perhaps presages, his death. Antigone's avian cry responds to his unburied dead body, on which birds feed.

Birds play all four roles in relation to Polyneikes's body. Polyneikes's avian cry, issued from his living body, prophetically announces the ensuing dramatic tragedy. His dead body is captured—captured as unburied—by the nets of Kreon's hommohumanistic edict. His corpse occasions Antigone's mother-bird cry as her response to its unburial. It also occasions a cannibalistic meal, of birds eating a bird body, which presages the avian feeding frenzy amid the failed augury.

All of these avian roles disturb. They unsettle. They do so in untranslatable ways. These kindred avian cries are unintelligible. The signs that they carry are of unintelligibility, incomprehensibility.

Indecipherable, they interrupt. Birds interrupt augury, as an avian message-delivery medium. Their messages cannot be delivered to Teiresias. They interrupt sacrifice, which Teiresias tries when augury fails. They interrupt prayer, so that human-animal messages are not delivered to gods.

Birds interrupt relationships, familial and political. Unpredictable and uncontrollable, they disrupt the political order. They remain outside hommohumanistic systems. In terms of hommohumanism, birds play *other* roles.

Birds also interrupt kinships. Their related roles suggest an avian counter-kinship: of Polyneikes and Antigone to birds, and so to one another. They relate to birds. (They, too, are interruptive and disruptive.) And they relate to one another as birds.

This avian relation changes their kinship positions. As humans, they are brother and sister. As birds, they become child and parent. Polyneikes becomes the baby bird missing from bird-mother Antigone's nest. He becomes the chick whose loss engenders her pained shriek of mourning. Antigone's mourning of Polyneikes doubles. She, as sister and mother, mourns his death, as brother and child.

Her mourning doubles. So does her kinship relation with Polyneikes. Their avian kinship does not dislodge their human kinship. The former supplements the latter. It offers a double counter-kinship, as avian and incestuous.

Antigone's counter-kinship doubles her mourning, her kinship ties—and, perhaps, her love for Polyneikes.

Human-animals follow birds in love. Birds are, Irigaray writes, "more advanced than we [human-animals] are in the amorous dialogue."[58]

Human-animals also follow birds in being. Birds make way for humanity. They humanize human-animals. They, Irigaray writes, "lead one's becoming," along "the pathway to restore but also transubstantiate the body, the flesh."[59] They reembody human-animals. They share (in) breath and give back to life. They might even work miracles.

If so, birds manifest their kinship with other others, on whom human-animals depend. These other others include other animals, angels, gods. Birds, Irigaray writes, "are our friends. But also our guides, our scouts. Our angels in some respect."[60]

So is Antigone.

Second Revival
Antigone the Angel

> I am convinced that paradigm shifts (and paradigm leaps to an even greater extent) occur in all the human sciences by incorporating a foreign element.
>
> — Roberto Esposito

> To stage the stakes of this work, I will once again take the figure of Antigone as my point of departure.
>
> — Luce Irigaray

Antigone is out of place.

Antigone is on the move. She moves *between*: *oikos* and *polis*, nature and culture, nonhuman and human, dead and living. She resides permanently in none of these positions. She remains, she says, "*metoikos*": a resident alien, a foreigner within.[1]

She remains on the move, displaced, between duties, desires, roles: of human sister and mother bird. She remains moving, *between*.

Antigone moves sexually. Her moves are in the feminine. They are through her femininity: filial or maternal, human or avian. Her feminine sexuality is the fluid medium of her movements. Her sexual sanguinity remains fluid, and flowing.

Her sexual fluid economy flows through (or overflows) bifurcations. These bifurcations often project an "other of the same" to prop up sameness, hommogeneity. They include schisms separating substance and semblance, matter and medium of exchange. Antigone's differential flows loosen(d) these schisms. These schisms become porous, passable, and Antigone passes through them.

Her passage exposes some, such as substance and semblance, as hommosexual erections. It undoes others, such as matter and medium of exchange. Matter is not static, fixed in place. Matter is, or becomes, a medium of exchange. These exchanges, these flows, are material.

Antigone's moves, in the feminine, are material. Her sexuality is substantial, but not stolid. It is dynamic, active, interactive. It is real, corporeal, reviving, revitalizing. Through it comes new form, new birth, new incarnation. Her sexuality, Luce Irigaray writes, "participates in the body's renaissance. And no other act is equivalent, in this sense. The most divine act."[2] It is corporeally *counter*-productive, and divinely so.

Her sexual fluidity means that Antigone remains open, dis-closed. She is neither contained nor container. Her place is never in place, not completely, not finally. Her place is place and interval. It is in flux.

Antigone comes in intervals. She works the interval.

An interval, a *diastēma*, is an opening, a threshold.[3] It comes *between*, as an entrance and a space between. An interval is a space that spaces. It enables passage. It is neither inside nor outside. Or it is both inside and outside.

An interval—*interval*—*inter*mediates. It comes between. It comes, for example, as an intermediary between potentiality and actuality, between potency and act. It comes between form and matter. It comes between times, between subjects, between bodies, between lovers. It comes between reality and possibility, and between possibilities. It comes between, as an opening. (It can also come as an opening *to*, between someone or something that is and someone or something that is not yet.)

An interval comes between, and differentiates. It delimits. It marks limits. It is the negative, or does its labor. With an interval comes difference(s).

An interval is like a hyphen. It touches. It brings differences into contact. Contact requires proximity. But proximity means distance, however small. And distance means difference(s).

An interval is a relation between differences. These relations are dynamic. They change, without collapsing. They maintain differences, but those differences can differ.

Living is intervallic. Living happens in intervals: between birth(s) and death(s), of whatever sorts. Living comes in this mortal interval. Living is breathing in this interval.

Antigone lives and moves between, *inter*. She *inter*-moves. Her moves are interstitial, interflowing, interceding, interactive, interruptive. She takes an *inter*course. She moves in passages. She comes in intervals.

Her inter-moves are intervallic. They open or pass through intervals.

Some of these inter-moves install internal intervals. She opens intervals on the inside. An internal interval comes between inside and inside, between an inside and itself. It makes a hole within a whole. It situates difference within sameness. It supplements: sameness with difference, or differance.

Other of Antigone's inter-moves occur in extant intervals. Moving in these intervals, she passes between inside and outside, and between outsides. She realizes contact: between inside and outside or between external others. She touches differences, makes differences touch.

Her intervallic inter-moves remain open. She touches her boundaries, her boundaries touch others, while keeping open. An interval is a space that, Irigaray writes, "is never closed. The limits touch while remaining open."[4]

Antigone touches on thresholds. She opens and keeps open threshold spaces. These thresholds are not minimums. They do not mark magnitudes or intensities that must be surpassed for something to happen. They are not lines to be crossed, in movements *from . . . to*.

These thresholds are openings, passageways. They are like doorframes or archways. They are between inside and outside, or between insides, or between outsides. They make way for movement. They allow multiple movements, within and across them.

These thresholds are *inter* and *trans*. They are relational spaces. They are where interactions take place.

They can be sites of hospitality. Hospitality names a receptive relation, of welcoming and offering to an other. It receives foreigners, strangers, others. It welcomes those who come, across differences. It lets them come.

It lets them come *as* foreigners, strangers, others. It welcomes their differences. It does not assimilate or modulate them. It does not "naturalize" them. Hospitality lets others come and remain other—and, so, continue to come. If an other comes and remains other, Jean-Luc Nancy writes, "as long as it remains . . . its coming does not cease: it continues to come."[5]

Hospitality happens in thresholds: between activity and passivity. Being hospitable means living in between. It means *letting come*.

Antigone touches on, stands in, moves through thresholds. (Other others do, too.) These thresholds are sexual, animal, moral, religious, living, loving. Antigone, for example, abides in an animal threshold: human-bird, marked by a hyphen.

These thresholds, these intervals, are interactive and even intersecting. Antigone, in her feminanimality, moves in sexual-animal thresholds. She moves in living-loving thresholds, between her beloved living and her beloved dead, between loving life and loving the dead. She moves in moral-religious thresholds, between obligations backed by gods. She moves in sexual-animal-religious thresholds, between animals and gods.

Antigone moves between animals and gods. She moves in human-divine intervals. In them, she passes between human-animals, between gods, and between human-animals and gods. She passes in human and divine intervals between her duties. (These intervals are also legal, between unwritten and written laws.) Her duties are plural: filial, religious, human, divine. These duties require and forbid her burial of Polyneikes's dead body.

In these intervals, she moves among kinships and counter-kinships. She moves among blood bonds, civil ties, vital links to the living. These last links, to the living, flow beyond human borders. They involve living with others, including the dead. The living live with the dead.

These links to the living are connections with others. These connections are cosmic. They are immanent and transcendent. The living live with the dead and the divine.

Living lives at the limits. Limits are where intervals come, where thresholds are, where others arrive.

Antigone lives among kinships. She lives and acts among others: Polyneikes, Kreon, Ismene, Haimon, Eteokles, Jokasta, Oedipus, Hades, Zeus.

Circulating amid duties and kinships, she moves amid desires. Antigone desires to live. She desires to live with others. She desires *inter*subjectivity. She desires to be a sister, to Ismene and Polyneikes (and Eteokles). She desires to bury her beloved. She desires to be pious, to Hades and Zeus. She desires to recognize limits, marked by the negative. She desires to end her suffering. She seems to desire to challenge Kreon's sovereignty. She even desires to go where she cannot: across livable limits.[6] These moves lead her to a mortal threshold. She is interred between life and death.

Moving among humans, Antigone moves between gods. She recognizes obligations to Hades and to Zeus. These gods are brothers, complements, sometimes doubles. To Hades, god of the underworld, she owes burial of her dead brother. Burial will enable his underworldly passage. To Zeus, god of the sky as well as protector of *oikos* and family, she also owes burial of her dead brother. Leaving Polyneikes's corpse unburied is doubly impious.[7]

(Antigone also acknowledges, as a child of incest, her blood-debt to Zeus. Zeus is still collecting, from her and her sister, for their parents' transgressions. As she tells Ismene, "of all the evils that descend from Oedipus / do you know one that Zeus does not fulfill for us, / the two still living?"[8])

Antigone recognizes this double impiety, and says so. She twice violates Kreon's edict forbidding Polyneikes's burial. She twice buries Polyneikes's corpse. Caught in the second act, a guard (who identifies her as a mother bird) brings her before Kreon. She admits her acts, and defends them. His edict, she claims, is unbinding because it is not bound to divine decree. "It was," she says, "not Zeus who made this proclamation; / nor was it Justice dwelling with the gods below / who set in place such laws as these for humankind."[9]

Antigone moves doubly, in two intervals: between gods and between human-animals and gods. She moves between Hades and Zeus, and she moves between them and Kreon (and Polyneikes). This former passage confirms her doubly divine backing. Both gods call for Polyneikes's burial. Neither god supports Kreon's edict forbidding his burial.

This revelation runs counter to Kreon's claimed alignment with Zeus. But his claim, Antigone announces, is empty. His edict is not divinely sanctioned. It is hommohumanistic. It challenges rather than honors divinities. As Antigone says, "nor did I think your proclamations had such strength / that, mortal as you are, you could outrun those laws / that are the gods', unwritten and unshakeable."[10] Antigone unveils Kreon's hommohumanism by passing between gods and between human-animals and gods.

Antigone's double inter-moves show that she does not "side" with Hades and her dead relatives against Kreon and Zeus. She "sides" with her dead relatives *and* with Hades *and* Zeus. She "sides" with her dead relatives because she moves between Hades and Zeus. They are all on the same side.

Antigone discloses her double duty. She is bound to bury Polyneikes's body and to maintain cosmic order, cosmic rhythms. She does the latter by doing the former. Antigone's duty to bury Polyneikes's body *is* her duty to the cosmos and its divinities.

Her double inter-moves double. Doing her double duty, Antigone maintains intervals, and passage between. She maintains, Irigaray writes, "a delicate balance between the two gods, the two worlds," as she endeavors "not to break a passage between the two worlds."[11] Antigone works to keep open thresholds, to maintain intervals of passage: for Polyneikes, for her, for the living, for the cosmos.

These passages are intertwining. They are binding, if not bounding. They are religious. Religious, Irigaray writes, "is the gesture which binds earth and sky, in us and outside of us," and between us.[12]

Antigone moves *between*, in doubly transcendent thresholds. She passes in intervals of vertical and horizontal transcendencies.[13] These transcendental intervals are relational. They are intervals allowing passage *between*. They allow passages between others. Transcendence comes in an other.

Vertical transcendences are relations with what is wholly other. (In religious traditions, the wholly other often becomes the holy other.) The wholly other is not an other, or an other other. It is simply other. It marks an absolute otherness, which remains inaccessible. It remains always *beyond*. It cannot be experienced or communicated with except on its terms. If the wholly other communicates, it is not *with*; it is *from* . . . *to*: from the wholly other to one (or many) among the living. These communiqués move in one direction.

Vertical transcendences are not interactive relations. They are not reciprocal or responsive. They are relations of incalculable distance, with what is infinitely other. They are relations of submission, subjugation, often sacrifice. They are frequently relations with gods or genealogies, which remain *beyond*, absent, unapproachable. Vertical transcendences correspond with "traditional" senses of transcendence. They are transcendentally transcendent.

Horizontal transcendences are relations with others. They take place between others, in intervals of difference. These intervals, and the differences they delimit, persist. They do not collapse. They might be large or small, or dynamic and changing. They might be abyssal. They might not be bridgeable. But they allow contact, touch, *inter*-action. Horizontal transcendences are relations *between*: between others who remain others. Their differences are irreducible. But they are not absolute.

Horizontal transcendences are immanently transcendent. They are immanent relations, occurring in a *here* and *now*, in proximity. They are relations with others, between others. These relations are reflexive and responsive. They are rhythmic, maybe even respiring. They are in-finite. They are transcendent because they respect limits and limitations. They respect the negative, and differences. They are immanent because they happen. They are *between*, not *beyond*.

Horizontal transcendences, immanently transcendent, are perhaps less *trans*cendences than *inter*scendences. They take place in intervals, in thresholds, in passages.

Horizontal transcendence opens onto sensible transcendence. Sensible transcendence is perceptible, palpable. It is real, corporeal. It happens, *here* and *now*. It comes in intervals, in spaces and touches, between bodies.

Sensible transcendence comes through corporeal senses—which are bodily openings to otherness. These senses mean that bodies *are* openings to differences, to otherness, to others. They mean that bodies are thresholds, sensible thresholds, always open.

Bodies live in relation. Bodies live with others. Sensible transcendence insists that *with* affects living. It insists that what a body lives *with* affects this body's living. It indicates that what is beyond a body, what is transcendent to it, shapes this body's living. Transcendence, what is beyond, is (at least partly) constitutive of bodily living. Bodies live sensibly, transcendentally.

Sensible transcendence requires sensitivity. To sense it requires being open to sensing it. Sensible transcendence requires openness: to what comes. It requires receptivity, to differences. It requires a sensible hospitality, to others who arrive. It requires being sensibly loosen(d)ed. It might call for corporeal edges to come a bit undone.

Sensible transcendence requires openness, for it comes as an opening. It is, Irigaray writes, "birth (in)to a transcendence, that of the other, still sensible, still physical and carnal, and already spiritual [*naissance à une transcendance, celle de l'autre, encore sensible, encore physique et charnelle, et déjà spirituelle*]."¹⁴

Sensible transcendence is a birth. It is a rebirth, a revival. It is a renewal of a life, of this life, here and now. It is life *encore*: not a different life, but life differently; not a new life, but life renewed. This renewal breathes new life into this life. This life is not left behind or exchanged for a new life. New life comes *in* this life. It comes in-finitely: as the infinite within the finite. This life is still finite, still mortal. But it is also something else, something more, something other. It is renewed, revived.

This renewal maintains life's vital mortality. It does not require passing through mortality *from* one life *to* another. This rebirth is a rebirth without an intervening death. It is a rebirth (in)to a reviving, revitalizing transcendence—one that is immanent, still sensible, still physical and carnal. This transcendence is, Irigaray writes, "a transcendence which now *remains* alive, sensible and even carnal. A transcendence that cannot be reduced to a mental idea or belief, but is incarnate, also in another"¹⁵ (my emphasis). It is a living transcendence, a material transcendence.

It is a transcendence. Sensible transcendence does not involve rebirth (in)to transcendence, undifferentiated and unlimited. This rebirth is (in)to *a* transcendence, one among many. This transcendence, like the embodied others it involves, is delimited by the negative.

This transcendence is not *beyond*. It is not otherworldly, or unearthly, or incorporeal, or ethereal. It is not eternal, or reincarnational, or transmigrational, or metempsychotic. This rebirth, this revival, takes place transcendentally here, transcendentally now. Its transcendence is inseparable from its immanence, its here-and-now-ness. It is inseparable from its embodiedness.

It is also inseparable from relation. This transcendence (in)to which this rebirth happens is other. It is an other transcendence. It is a transcendence of an other—*an* other, not the wholly other. This other is not abstract or ideal. This other, he or she, is real, corporeal, carnal, sensible—and sexual. This other, he or she, is embodied, and therefore sexual. Sensible transcendence occurs sexually, through sexualities.

This other, he or she, is sensible, physical, carnal, corporeal. So is the transcendence that comes between them. It comes *between* them, and remains: irreducible, unclosable, *between* them. This transcendence is inter-active. It involves a material interaction. It engenders corporeal communication, sensual contact, sensible exchange. It engenders a synesthetic interval, where rebirth comes, through interaction. This transcendence happens between others who are sensible, physical, carnal—who are finite, and living. It comes in the space of the negative, between their finite corporealities. It comes in between finitudes. It is in-finite. It comes in infinite intervals.

It is in-finite, corporeal, and already spiritual. Spiritual does not signify incorporeal or decorporeal. Spirit is not opposed to corporeality. Spirit *is* corporeal, and intercorporeal. It is living, breathing. Spirit, *spiritus*, means breath. To be spiritual is to be breathing. To be already spiritual is to be already breathing. To be sensibly transcendentally spiritual is to be breathing with an other, to be respiring together, to have air flowing between.

Sensible transcendence is a rebirth—an opening and a passage—(in)to sensibly interactive relations with an other or others. (Sensible transcendence, like other and difference, is in the plural.) It takes place in corporeal and intercorporeal intervals. It touches on bodies, coming between them. Its touches are sensible, physical, carnal, spiritual. They are passages of living and breathing.

They are also passages of ethics and ontology. Sensible transcendence is an ethical experience of an other, and of an other's transcendence. Neither an other nor an other's transcendence is appropriable. An other, as transcendent, remains irreducibly different. This difference(s) remains unknown. Others can interact, touch, contact, exchange, share.

Sensible transcendence occasions these interactions. It occasions an ethics of approach: approaching an other, approaching the unknown. This approach must be open, as an opening to an other and to the unknown. Approaching the unknown (other) means approaching in(to) the dark. It means not knowing what is coming. It requires becoming receptive, hospitable, vulnerable. It requires becoming loosen(d)ed.

Such an ethics of approaching the unknown (other) is a mystical ethics. "Mystical" comes from *mustikos*, which means mystery. Mystical names what is unknown, unseen—which is where this ethics leads.[16] It retraces the negative, as limit and limitation of what is known. Mystical expresses a knowing humility: an admission of the unknown.

Mystical also names a religious humility, a path toward a divine unknown. This path is negative. It is apophatic. Advancing along it, into the dark, calls for ethical humility. It calls for self-loosen(d)ing, self-undoing, to make way for an other experience, of an other transcendence.

This transcendence is sensible, sensual, excentric, ecstatic. It is corporeally spiritual, inter-active, in-finite, renewing, rebirthing. It is, Irigaray writes, "never the same, always new. Never repeated or repeatable."[17]

Sensible transcendence calls for an embodied ethics of proximity. It calls for a sensible, sexual ethics of intervals, which maintain difference(s) and allow contact. These intervals connect others without collapsing their differences. These intervals preserve plurality.

Ontology, too, passes through these intervals. Being no longer lives in a neutered, neutralized "there is," or "*il y a.*" (The latter reveals that such neutrality is not neutral. It is already sexual. Its claim to neutrality is made as a "naturalizing" effort by, and for, hommosexuality.)

These sensible transcendental thresholds, these interactive ethical intervals, make way for an other way of living with, of being with, others. They make way, Irigaray writes, "for a 'we are' or 'we become,' 'we live here' together," by "opening to a *sensible transcendental* happening through us [*advenant à travers nous*]."[18]

"We are" and "we become" are ways of saying " 'we live here' together." We means *with*. It means *with others*. It means living, being, becoming: plurally, relationally.

An embodied ethics of passage and proximity is what Antigone desires, and performs. Antigone exemplifies "'we live here' together," with others. Her duties, her decisions, her deeds are about living together, with others. They enactively seek a sexual, corporeal ethics of proximities. These proximities would come in cosmic, mortal, animal, and divine intervals. They would relate the living and the dead, the human and the nonhuman, the human-animal and the divine. They would do so sexually, sensibly, transcendentally.

Sensible transcendence *happens*, between and through us. It is what happens, what comes, what arrives. It is an event. An event *is* what happens, what comes, what arrives. An event names what is "incoming," without notice. An event is when the unexpectable occurs, when the unforeseeable shows up, when the impossible happens. An event is another name for a miracle: when the impossible happens, here and now, as a living experience, arriving in a sensible transcendental interval.

Sensible transcendence happens, *between* and *through* us. It is intermediate. It comes, Irigaray writes, as "intermediate [*intermédiaire*]. Neither the one nor the other. Not neutral or neuter for all that. Forgotten ground of our condition between mortals and immortals, humans and gods, creatures and creators. In us and between us."[19] Sensible transcendence is an *inter*mediate *inter*val of *inter*actions among others. These interactions can be vertically or horizontally transcendent. But they come through sensible transcendence: *between* before *beyond*.

Sensible transcendence happens, between and through us, as an opening: an opening *to*. This sensible transcendental opening is to the divine. Sensible transcendence is the way of divinity. It is a divine threshold. It makes way, in a human-divine interval. What comes, what happens, through this sensible transcendental interval is divinity.

Divinity is reviving. It brings a revival, but not of a god. It brings a revival of divinity "through us": by, Irigaray writes, "suscitating it through us [*le suscitant à travers nous*], among us, as resurrection or transfiguration of blood, of flesh, by their language and their ethics."[20] It brings a revival of "us" through divinity—through a corporeal language and ethics, of blood and body. Divinity comes through "us," among "us." It comes in relation: *with* and *to*. It comes in revival, rebirth, resurrection. This revival transfigures blood and body, on their terms. Divinity comes in terms of blood and body. Its language and ethics are bloody and bodily.

Divinity comes as a bodily event. It comes as an event that occurs through and among bodies. It comes thanks to bodily porosities, through which corporeal revivals arrive.

Divinity names a sensible transcendence. It comes through intervals, and revives. It comes through living, and for life. It comes through blood and bodies: sexual, corporeal, finite, interactive, breathing.

Divinity is not god. "God" remains vertically transcendent, transcendentally transcendental, inaccessibly *beyond*. Divinity happens, arrives, through a sensible transcendental threshold.

So does an angel. An angel comes in sensible transcendental intervals, *between*. An angel is an agent of sensible transcendence, in human-divine intervals. An angel is a figure of the threshold.

Antigone is on the move. She passes between humans, between gods, between gods and humans, between nonhuman-animals and human-animals. She moves vertically transcendentally and horizontally transcendentally. She does so through intervals of sensible transcendence. She abides at *inter*sections of transcendental thresholds. She lives in sensibly transcendent intervals, where horizontal and vertical transcendencies touch, cross.

Her moves exemplify, or perform, religion as a passage and relation *between*. Religion, Antigone shows, is about relation, which requires movement.

These moves make Antigone even more difficult to contain or corral. A dialectic cannot do it. She flows between *either . . . or*, and she does not end in sublating resolution. She is, for example, neither master nor slave. She is undialectizable and undigestable.

She crosses dialectic flows, confounding their currents. She exposes porosities and remains porous, open. She moves among the living (and the dead), between animalities and divinities.

Antigone comes in intervals. She lives in *between*. She moves in an animal interval: human-bird (marked by a hyphen). She moves in a mortal interval: living-dead. She moves in an angelic interval: animal-divine.

Antigone is an angel.

An angel is on the move. An angel moves in all directions: horizontal, vertical, diagonal, spiral. An angel moves through intervals of space and time. An angel crosses space and time in passing between places. An angel is always moving, to an other place. An angel is always departing again.

An angel is a moving messenger, a messenger on the move. An angel moves, and moves messages. An angel is messaging. An angel deals in messages.

"Angel" means message. *Angelia*, in Greek, means message, tiding, proclamation, news. *Angelō* is a Greek verb meaning to bear a message, to announce, to proclaim, to report. *Angelos* is Greek for messenger, envoy, announcer (especially of birds, in augury).

Angelos is also the name of a Greek goddess. Daughter of Zeus and Hera, Angelos becomes a deity of the underworld. Some mythological lines entwine her with Artemis, a goddess of wild animals, childbirth, virginity. Some (other) mythological lines entwine her with Hekatē, a goddess associated with crossroads, entranceways, thresholds. (Hekatē is also mother of angels.) Angelos, like Antigone, is in relation: with nonhuman and human (feminine) animals, with virgins and mothers, with intervals and intersections. Angelos, like Antigone, is in relation: in intersections, thresholds, intervals, passages.

Antigone might become *angelos* doubly: as an angel and as a divinity.

An angel is a bearer of messages and relationships. An angel bears, brings, carries, delivers: messages and relationships. An angel moves in animal-divine intervals, *between* humans and gods. An angel goes both ways. An angel comes and goes, arrives and departs, proceeds and returns, *excedit* and *redit*.

Angelic moves are relational. An angel *inter*poses, Irigaray writes, "to allow and preserve, to allow preserving the relation, the liaison."[21] "To allow and preserve" is to open and keep open, to let come, to maintain relations and relational intertwinings.

Delivering messages, angels are intermediary, coming *between* humans and gods. Their moves bear out these relations. They interweave humans and gods. They weave double relations: between a human and a god (between receiver and sender), and between a human and an angel (between receiver and deliverer).

These relational weaves are an angel's identity. Angelic identity is thoroughly relational. It comes between. It *is* on the way.

An angel is (also) an *angeion*, a vessel. A vessel gives place. It gives place to what it bears. In giving place, it gives hospitality, to an other, in relation. It bears an other as other, without collapsing differences. It bears difference(s), and delivers.

Angelic delivery is a counter-maternity.

An angel, an *angeion*, is a kind of *khōra*. *Khōra* names a space *between*: between places and times, between here-now and there-then. It comes as a third term, between matter and form.[22] It comes in an interval between them. It is sensible and transcendental. *Khōra* offers, Plato writes, a space "for all that has birth," that arrives through birth; it is "the wet-nurse of becoming," flowing through the elements.[23] *Khōra* gives birth, through a counter-maternity: without collapsing into the maternalfeminine. *Khōra* gives birth otherwise.

It delivers differently, like an angel. This angelic vessel, this *khōral* angel, delivers what it bears upon arrival. An angel, as a vessel, is a medium for a message.

An angelic message is formative, and forming. It delivers substantially, in its contents. It also delivers practically, in its effects. An angelic message forms. It informs, proforms, deforms, reforms, transforms its recipient. (A proform is a lexical unit, such as a pronoun, whose meaning depends on reference to some other part of the context or sentence in which it occurs. To proform is to form in context: in space, in time, in relation.)

An angelic message also performs. An angelic message and the messaging angel are *pol*yperformative. An angel delivers a message and is a message. An angel transmits a message and performs a message. An angel's transmission is a performative message. It performs passage, *inter* and *trans*, as ways of relating with others. It performs between intervals, and across enclosures. An angel, in transmission, transgresses enclosures.

In doing so, an angel performatively tells of a passage between envelopes: of gods and of human-animals. An angel moves in this passage, between and across envelopes. An angel, Irigaray writes, "is one who unceasingly *traverses the envelope*, the envelopes, goes from one side to the other, alters every deadline [*échéance*], every decision, thwarts [*déjoue*] every repetition."[24] These traversals induce and deliver these effects. Altering every decision, they inform ethics. Changing every deadline, they reform space and time.[25] Thwarting every repetition, they deform returns to the same, the self-same.

They effect, Irigaray writes, "change[s] in the perception and conception of *space-time*, the *inhabiting* of places and of *envelopes of identity*."[26] The envelopes that an angel unceasingly traverses are of identities. An angelic identity is relational. It *is* in transit. It *is* a deliverer and a delivery. It is *as* a messenger, a message. These delivered messages are (in part) of relational possibilities.

An angel moves through envelopes that would envelope, that would seal, identities. The message envelopes that an angel delivers are to be unsealed, opened, and not reclosed. The identity envelopes that an angel traverses are, too. These openings are dis-closures. They have effects. They make way for passage, for traversals. They also affect deadlines and decisions dependent upon (and repetitions dictated by) these envelopes' seals.

Opening these envelopes opens new ways of conceiving and perceiving, of living and moving, in space-time and place. Opening envelopes of identity opens space-time and place.[27] It opens them *to* what comes, and *to* what might come.

It undoes them. Once opened, these envelopes do not reseal. They remain open.

Through these open envelopes can come an angelic message. Through them can come an angel—bearer of messages and relations, of performances and formations, of traversals and disclosures—bearing a relational message. Through them an angel can deliver and disclose a sensible transcendental ethics.

This sensible transcendental ethics would be one of loosen(d)ing. It would bring an ethical loosen(d)ing of identity-envelopes. This loosen(d)ing would disclose immobile identities. It would unseal human-animals from these enveloping containments. It would enable movement, flux, formation. It would make way for in-finite movement between places, passage toward others, proximity, contact. It would engender new relational possibilities: new proximities, new contacts, new intertwinings, with other others. It would open intervals for embodied human-animals to move like angels.

These traversed, disclosed identity-envelopes are human-animal and divine. By passing between and across them, an angel performatively proclaims this passage's possibility. An angel performatively announces that sexual, corporeal human-animals can make this passage, move in this interval.

An angel, by traversing envelopes, bears a relational message. This message performs plural relations. These relations are between sender and receiver (for example, a god and a human-animal). They are between deliverer and receiver (an angel and a human-animal). They are between receiver and receiver (between a human-animal and himself or herself.) An angel's message is, comes as, a re(ve)lation.

Antigone's angelic messages come as re(ve)lations. Her angelic messages are definitely formative. They deform existing natural-cultural flows of hommohumanism. They reform relations across civil and familial lines. They inform Kreon, and everyone else, that Kreon's actions lack divine backing. They transform Kreon's sovereign response, which transforms everything that tragically follows.

Passing between human-animal and divine others, Antigone moves like an angel. She traverses envelopes. She flows through intervals in an *angeion*. She moves *between*. She moves between god, man, and woman—between gods, paternalmasculine men, and maternalfeminine women.[28] Antigone fits into none of these envelopes of identity. But she moves *between* them as she passes *between* the dead and the living, the human-animal and the divine. She traverses these identity-envelopes, flowing through them.

Antigone is not an envelope. She is not posted, sent, delivered. She is not a message. She is a messenger.[29] She is a mail carrier in this in-finite, sensibly transcendental postal system. She is an angel.

Angels are in motion and in flux. An angel is a messenger, who is never immobile, never enclosed, never closing. An angel discloses enclosures, reopening them, to allow passage.

Angels, moving messengers, are *poly*-performers. In bearing messages, angels perform plurally. They move, or transit. They pass, and are in passage. They deliver. They announce.[30] They interpret. They discern, especially between good and evil. They assist. They reveal. They give. They love.

Angels illumine. They are light. (They move at least as fast.) Light comes *between*, intermediately. It gives way to visibility. It gives to be seen. It is a medium for sensible experience.

Angels open. They reopen and keep open. They are dis-closing. They are always reopening intervals, to allow passage. Angels are key(s).

As *poly*-performers, angels are polymorphic. An angel might be cast, or recast, as an other messenger: a mail carrier, a postman or postwoman, a singing messenger, a newscaster. An angel might also be recast as a traveler, a translator, a pilot, a ladder, a dancer, a guardian, a breath of wind, a flux, a preposition, a professor, an interchange, an interlacer, an instant message, a light, a network, a newborn, a cartographer, a skeleton key.

Angels, Michel Serres writes, "are individual and multiple; messengers that both appear and disappear; visible and invisible; constructive of messages and message-bearing systems; spirit and body; spiritual and physical; of two sexes and of none; natural and manufactured; collective and social; both orderly and disorderly; producers of noise, music, and language; intermediaries and interchangers."[31]

Angels inextricate. They entwine, enmesh. They illuminate that kataphatic and apophatic—positive and negative, light and dark—paths between humans and gods are inextricable. They represent inextricable links between immanence and transcendence, between sensibility and ineffability. They deliver gifts of light and lead into divine darkness. They make way, doubly.

Angels deliver relationally. These deliverers and their deliveries, of a sensible transcendental ethics, would deliver sexually and corporeally.

Angels make way for sexual, corporeal, human-animal passages. Human-animals can move like angels. They can pass between envelopes of the divine and of the human-animal-living-cosmic.[32] They can do so thanks to angels. Angels open and keep open these possible passages. They deliver the message that these passages are possible.

These passages are unenveloping traversals. They unenvelop identities, allowing movement between. These unenveloping traversals are sexual and corporeal acts. They move across envelopes, through intervals, between thresholds that are sexual and corporeal. They pass through sexual and corporeal intervals. The envelopes that angels unceasingly traverse are sexual and corporeal.

An angel delivers, sexually and corporeally.

An angel, as an *angeion*, is a corporeal vessel, a carnal interval. An *angeion* names a bodily opening, such as a vein or a lung.[33] Vein and lung are open intervals. They are thresholds, through which blood and breath pass. They are spaces for movement. And these spaces move. A vessel is, Aristotle writes, "a transportable place [*topos metaphorētos*]"—a *trans*portable place.³⁴ It transits between thresholds. It gives place in motion.

An angel, a corporeal vessel, delivers a sexual message. An angel delivers a sexuality not yet corporealized. It is, Irigaray writes, "as if the angel were a figuration of a sexuality never yet incarnated. Of a light, divine gesture (or tale) of flesh not yet acted, flourished. Always fallen or awaiting parousia."³⁵

An angel delivers an other parousia.

Parousia is a Greek name for presence, or arrival. It names an advent: an arrival, a coming to be here and now, of someone or something (an object or an event). Its root, *ousia*, signifies being materially. *Ousia* is a word for being, but as material substance rather than as (only) ideal form. Parousia would be a substantial arrival, a material advent. Parousia would come corporeally. It would arrive through a bodily threshold.

An other parousia would be an other way of being bodily (sexually and corporeally). It would be an other way of being *bodily*, and of *being* bodily. It would be an other way of being *bodily*, in (ethical) relation to others. It would be an other way of *being* bodily, an inventive (ontological) possibility for living.

These inventive openings entwine, ethically and ontologically. With an other parousia would come an other *paraousia*. Parousia names a way of being bodily. *Paraousia* names a way of being bodily beside, alongside, others. (In Greek, *para* means beside, alongside, near, by.) A *paraousia* would be a parousia of proximity, of embodied, proximate living.³⁶

An other parousia would bring an other way of bodily being in relation: of living, with others. An angel delivers an other way of being, sexually and corporeally. This delivery is double. An angel delivers a doubly other parousia.

An angel moves *between*, in intervals. An angel traverses envelopes. An angel also makes way for human-animals to move in these intervals, traverse these envelopes. An angel's passage lets human-animals pass. An angel moves and lets others move. An angel performs a double movement, delivers a double message.

So, too, with parousia. An angel delivers an angelic parousia. An angel also delivers a possibility for an other parousia, a human-animal parousia. An angel delivers an angelic way of being, sexually and corporeally, *and* an other way for human-animals to be, sexually and corporeally.

An other parousia would bring an other sexual and corporeal ethics. "A sexual or carnal ethics," Irigaray writes, "would demand that both angel and body may be found [or may find themselves] together."[37] These findings, and their ensuing deliveries, might be double.

1. This other sexual-carnal-ethical parousia might come when and where an angel and a human-animal body find themselves together, in a sensibly transcendental threshold. When angel and human-animal body are proximate, an other ethics arrives. Angel and human-animal body would relate, touch, entwine, and so engender an other ethics. This other ethics would be an ethics of proximity and passage. It would be an intervallic ethics, coming in an animal-angel interval. It would arrive, and be, *between.*

This sexual-corporeal ethics would materialize in mucous. Mucous is *between.* It is not quite solid, and not quite liquid. It is between solid and liquid.

Mucous comes *between.* It comes in bodily membranes: corporeal openings. It lines membranous passages, mucosae, through which a body communicates, interacts, with air. It lines passages through which air passes, in and out. It lines passages through which a body breathes. These living passages are respiratory, alimentary, and genitourinary. They are the passages of life, the passages that engender and sustain living. (These passages are sexuate. They differ with sexual differences, and their genitourinary variations. They are procreative passages that induce and deliver [new] life.)

Mucous comes *between* differences, in corporeal and sexual thresholds. It abides where bodies encounter living differences. Thinking through these differences means thinking through mucous. Thinking through mucous is necessary for delivering other ethical possibilities: other ways for bodies to live in relation.[38]

Mucous comes *between*, like an angel. It brings an other parousia: of the divine. Mucous, Irigaray writes, "would call for the return or the arrival of the god in a new incarnation, an other parousia."[39] This other, embodied, divine parousia would come through mucous. Mucous would be the medium for this other parousial arrival. It would line the material threshold of, Irigaray writes, an "opening to a sensible transcendental happening through us."[40]

Angelic materiality might be mucous. Mucous might deliver the divine.

Antigone's sexual materiality is blood-y, never milk-y. She is filial-feminine: sisterly, and singularly sanguine. Her fluidity would remain singular and sanguine. As an angel, mucous would supplement her materiality. As an angel, Antigone would be blood-y *and* mucous-y. She would pass through two corporeal media, in sexual and angelic thresholds, between human and divine. She would move through blood and mucous.

She would deliver (perhaps through her counter-maternity) an other parousia, through her sisterly sexual difference. Her filial-femininity would engender an other ethical parousia: of desire. This parousia would be of a sexualized or sexually sensible transcendence by way of desire. It would open thresholds of desire for parousial passage, through sexual differences. Sexual differences and sexual desire would make way for an other ethical parousia, an other way of living with others. (Antigone's filial-femininity would be one such way.)

This other relational parousia would come through a sexualized sensible transcendence. It would come through mucous, as a medium of parousia.

This other relational parousia would also come through a sensibly transcendental *erōs*. It would come through an other *erōs*, an angelic *erōs*. This *erōs* would come, would transpire, in intervals: in movements and modes. These intervallic movements and modes would involve wonder, in the affective mode; touch, in the sensuous mode; transgression, in the subjective mode; fluidity, in the elemental mode; and future, in the temporal mode.[41] This angelic *erōs* manifests movements in a sexual-corporeal ethics of parousia. It entwines sexuality and corporeality with *erōs*.

Antigone performs this entwining exceptionally. Her *erōs* is exceptional. It is for the impossible.[42] The impossible names what has not arrived, what has not yet been delivered. It traverses distances and envelopes. It names what may be still to come (however impossibly).

> 2. This other sexual-carnal-ethical parousia might also, or instead, come when disembodied angel and angelic body find themselves together. It might arrive when an angel becomes embodied. This parousia might be of an angelic body: an other kind of body. When this other, angelic body arrives, so does an other ethics. It would be an ethics of an other embodiment, an other way of being bodily.

With this other parousia—of angelic embodiment and sexual-carnal ethics—would come other sexualities. Angelic bodies would embody angelic sexualities. They would pass through, arrive in, a sexual-carnal threshold. A sexual-carnal ethics would come through this threshold. It would be delivered in other, angelic sexualities. (These angelic sexualities might be ethically inventive for human-animals.) It would deliver a new relational possibility: of a couple, as angel and human-animal.

This couple would invite others beyond (hommohumanistic) genealogies' vertically transcendental determinisms. They would invent other genealogical possibilities. They would welcome, and welcome others to, Irigaray writes, "a time of a theology of the breath in its horizontal and vertical becoming."[43] They would welcome, and welcome others to, a sensible transcendental theology of breath, of the living.

A sensible transcendental theology of breath would deliver an other sense of "theology." It would deliver an other parousia of the divine, through a sexual-corporeal threshold.

Theology, coming from its Greek progenitors *theos* and *logos*, typically signifies words (*logos*) about god (*theos*). This sense of theology is theo-logical. It unfolds a logic of god. In this sense, theology is about (a) god. But a sensible transcendental theology of breath would deliver a *theios-logos*: words about, and a logic of, the divine (*theios*).[44] And this divine would be different from god. A *theios-logos* would not collapse divinity, a way of being, into a divine being. It would not bind divinity to a god.

The envelope of divine identity would be traversed, left open. "God" would be unenveloped, disclosed. The name "God" would no longer name a being. It would name intervals: of space-time, between places. It would name spacing. It would make way for differences. "God" would make way for thinking, and living, through these differences, by rethinking space and time, being and relation. "God," Agnes Bosanquet writes, would be "a term by which we can experience a sensible transcendental."[45] "God" would name a sensible transcendental threshold. This sensible transcendental threshold would be a way of becoming divine.

"God" would no longer name a divine being. "God" would name a way of becoming divine.

Angels move through openings. They move through divinely interactive intervals. They make way for becoming divine. An other parousia would deliver a way of becoming divine.

Becoming divine does not mean becoming a divinity. It does not mean becoming a god or goddess. Becoming divine names a way of living: in relation, with others.

Becoming divine is a matter of living. It is a matter of living, openly, *with*. It involves living openly with others, and other others, through interactive intervals of difference(s).

Second Revival

Becoming divine does not mean becoming godlike. But it might mean becoming angelic. Angels are divinely other others who *inter*act. Angels move between, pass through, cross over confining boundaries. They move, pass, cross without domination, without violating an other. They respect differences and abide by the negative.

As *poly*-performers, angels disclose identities. They recast themselves, depending on singular instances of relation. They recast themselves in relation(s) to sender, receiver, message, context. They are *poly*relational, in intervals of differences. They are openings.

Becoming angelic would be trans-formative. It would trans-form human ways of living: of being with and relating to. These trans-formations would be inter-acting and re-incarnating. They, like angels, would bare new bodily openings. They would disclose new corporeal possibilities. They would deliver an other parousia, with an other sexual-corporeal ethics.

Becoming angelic would involve living in a sensible transcendental interval. It would involve opening and keeping open sensual passages: respirative, receptive vessels lined with mucous. It would involve unenveloping identities. It would involve hospitable, vulnerable exposure to what comes. Becoming angelic would require becoming perpetually porous. It would require continual self-loosen(d)ing. It would call for becoming undone, and unveiled. Becoming angelic would mean that the unveiling of divinity and of differences—"god" and "other"—would, Irigaray writes, "necessitate my 'proper' unveiling. . . . Let this be an act I would be capable of, without ever having done with it."[46]

Becoming angelic would take place through angelization. Angelization names, Steven Chase writes, an interval "between humanity and divinity that, requiring them both to dwell as they are, is nonetheless a new creature of their joint creation."[47] Angelization would be an other parousia, a co-creative opening that makes way for a new creature, a new creation, a new sensibly transcendental horizon(tal).

Becoming angelic would be a way of becoming divine.

Becoming divine names an opening *to*. Becoming divine calls for loosen(d)ing identity envelopes and opening *to* others, differences, intervals, passages, arrivals. It entails receptivity, vulnerability, interaction, formation. Becoming divine means living in-trans-formation. Becoming divine is a way of living with others. It is for life.

Antigone's movements in intervals would herald her other parousia. Antigone becomes angelic. In doing so, she becomes divine. She incarnates an other sexuality, an other way of being bodily, and other ways of relating. She traverses envelopes of identity. She moves through sexual and corporeal and vital differences. She moves between, opening and keeping open thresholds and possibilities of passage. She moves among the living. She breathes with the living, amid their differences. She is with others, for others. She is with the living, and for life.

An other parousia discloses other sensibly transcendental possibilities. It discloses other sensibly transcendental horizons. These horizons offer possibilities of what is to come. These horizons are of the future.
Antigone is, too.

Third Revival
Antigone the Future

> Ultimately, this book offers a theory of queer futurity that is attentive to the past for the purposes of critiquing a present.
>
> — José Esteban Muñoz

> To stage the stakes of this work, I will once again take the figure of Antigone as my point of departure.
>
> — Luce Irigaray

Antigone is out of time.
    Yet she lives on. She is revived, repeatedly. Revived, she becomes an animal. Revived again, she becomes an angel. Revived once more, she comes as a prophet.
    A prophet moves through time, like an angel moves through space.
    An angel moves between spaces to deliver messages. An angel moves between here and there: arriving and departing, arriving anew and departing again. An angel moves messages between places and persons. An angel moves *inter locos, inter personas*. An angel commutes, communicates, communes. An angel relays and relates, between differences. An angel delivers messages that affect, or effect, relations. An angel heralds an arrival, of something new.
    A prophet moves between times to deliver messages. A prophet moves *inter tempora*. A prophet moves between now and

then. A prophet delivers a message, now, about what is to come, then—in the future. A prophet tells the future. A prophet tells the future in the present, and to the present.

A prophet is of the future.

A prophet, like an angel, delivers a message. This delivery is a redelivery. A prophet, like an angel, receives a message to be delivered. A prophet receives a message, from an other, to be delivered, to an other other (or others). This prophetic delivery redelivers what was delivered to this prophet. This message is not a prophetic invention. It is a prophetic retransmission. A prophet, like an angel, is a medium for a message. A prophet, like an angel, receives and delivers.

This message might come prepackaged, as a message. It might come, for example, directly from a god or goddess. If so, this prophet *is* an angel. This message might instead require translation, interpretation. It might require divining. It might come, for example, indirectly through augury, or an oracular sign, or a presentiment, or a faithful commitment. If so, a prophet is sensitive, and inventive: he or she receives what is incoming (*in-venire*) and translates it before delivering it.

Antigone plays both prophetic roles. She is an angel-prophet, who delivers messages between domains: of the divine, the dead, the living. When, for example, Kreon justifies his unequal treatment of Eteokles's and Polyneikes's corpses, Antigone intervenes with a message: "despite that, Hades longs to see these laws fulfilled."[1]

She is also a sensitive and inventive prophet. She foresees and foretells. She presages, for example, her death. She tells Ismene and Kreon that "my soul has long since / been dead, that I might offer help to those who died."[2] Approaching her tomb, she says to the chorus, "no wedding hymn is my lot; / no marriage song sung for me; / no, I shall be Akheron's bride."[3] She announces in the present what will come to be in the future. She divines her destiny.

In Sophokles's tragedy, she plays the prophet. She is recast as a prophet, on whom the prophet Teiresias depends. He is unable to divine a message through augury or sacrifice. The birds necessary for augury make noises never heard before. The birds necessary for sacrifice burst organs and ooze fat, putting out the sacrificial fire. Based on these failed rites, Teiresias offers a diagnosis rather than a prophecy. He cites Kreon's edict forbidding Polyneikes's burial as "why the gods accept our sacrificial / prayers no more, nor flames from burning victims' thighs, / nor do the birds scream cries that give me signs."[4]

Teiresias does make an inventive prophecy, based on signs: from Antigone. Antigone is the sign that Teiresias interprets. (Her avian cry is the one bird scream that gives a sign.) He perceives her filial dutifulness, her desire for cosmic order, her pieties to Hades and to Zeus, and her impassioned defense of these commitments.

In these actions Teiresias divines Kreon's crimes: "you've cast below a person / who belongs above, making a living soul / reside within a tomb dishonorably, and keep / up here a corpse belonging to the gods below, / deprived of rites, of offerings, of piety."[5] From these signs Teiresias interprets and delivers his prophecy to Kreon: "you shall not live through many more / swift-racing courses of the sun before you give / a child of your own flesh and blood in turn, a corpse / to pay for corpses."[6] Teiresias's prophecy turns out to be right. Haimon's death soon follows his prophetic soothsaying.

A prophet gives place to what will take place. A prophet reconfigures time-space and place. Foretelling what is to come, a prophet preplaces a future in a present. When this future takes place, happens in its present, its taking place is a replacement, of what has already come in its place.

A prophet comes in the future anterior. The future anterior tells what will have been. It names an act or event that has not happened but will have happened by a particular point in the future.

The future anterior is a prophetic tense. It speaks in a prophetic voice—or a prophetic voice speaks in the future anterior. It, like a prophet, shuttles between times. It moves between a present, the temporal scene of its statement; a future, a horizonal point on its temporal trajectory; and a future that will have become past—a future that will have happened—by that horizonal point in time.

A prophet delivers a message in the future anterior. A prophet, like an angel, announces what, at a future point, will have happened—but what, presently, has not yet happened. A prophetic announcement will, in the future, be *already*. But this announcement is, in the present, *not yet*. A prophet moves between *already* and *not yet*.

Antigone, prophet, moves between *already* and *not yet*. But she is not only between. Antigone, coming from the past, is already. Antigone, coming from (or persisting into) the future, is not yet. She instantiates these locales and transits in the interval between them. She is *already* and *not yet* and *between*.

She persists, *inter tempora*. She persists, *trans tempora*. Her persistence, Irigaray writes, "is linked to our History more than the usual interpretations claim, even though it has not yet entered into History and still represents today a question."[7] Antigone already has a place in history and is not yet in history. She already has a place in history but does not yet reside there.

Why? Because she remains *between*. Because she remains undialectizable, undigestible, unsublatable. Because she remains recastable, redoubtable, revivable and reviving. Because she remains not yet unveiled. Her unveiling remains to come.[8] It has yet to happen, yet to arrive.

A prophet announces an arrival that has not yet arrived. A prophet does the impossible.

A prophet foretells what has not yet happened. A prophet *for*-tells. *For* marks a temporal interval between present and future. It marks a threshold through which a future passes, and comes to pass. *For* makes way for the future to come. "This 'for,' this *pro*-," Jacques Derrida writes, "would become the prolegomenon of everything. . . . Absolute prerequisite, the *pro* of *for* pronames thus and prenames everything."⁹ By *for*-telling, prophet and prophecy become temporal thresholds, transiting present and future. Prophet and prophecy open and keep open present to future. Prophet and prophecy give way—like angels.

They give way *for* life. Among the living, *for* is *for life*. *For*, Derrida writes, "conditions the meaning of 'life.' "¹⁰ Life, like time, comes by way of *for*.

Antigone is *for*. She is *for* life, *for* the dead, *for* living with the dead, *for* the divine, *for* desire, *for* difference(s), *for* others, *for* the future. She *for*-tells the future.

She does so from both directions, going both ways: past and future. She comes from the past and from the future. She is a prophetic predecessor from the future. These predecessors, Irigaray writes, "have no future. They come from the future. In them, it is already present."¹¹

Antigone performatively prophesies a counter-humanity. She prophetically performs, in her fifth-century-BCE context, a counter-humanity that has not yet come (except through her).

Her feminanimality bleeds together sexuality and corporeality. It binds them for life, with blood and mucous.

Her filial-femininity vitalizes a different sexual difference. It no longer inters femininity in maternity.

Her filial-feminanimality makes way for a counter-maternity. A counter-maternity delivers a counter-humanity that overflows hommohumanistic erections.

This counter-humanity lives among the living. It breathes hospitably with others, in reflexive respirations. It animates a polyzoontopolitics. It comes, in Roberto Esposito's words, as 'the achievement of a state never before experienced . . . it is a way of being human that is no longer defined in terms of alterity from our animal origins."¹²

Antigone's filial-feminanimal angelic counter-humanity delivers messages. These messages announce inter-relational possibilities among others. They herald ways of living, and living *with*.

Her angelic passages open intervals, in space and time, place and identity. Through them come messages and movement and inter-action. These passages and her angelization inter-relate the human-animal and the divine through sensible transcendental thresholds. They dis-close an other parousia, a path of becoming divine. They announce, Irigaray writes, "mediation, mediators, news concerning the place where the divine presence would be held . . . of its awaiting and of its return."[13]

Her prophetic pronouncements call *for* the future. They announce *already* what remains *not yet*. They unveil what remains unforeseeable. They perdure, persist, insist. They survive, awaiting a mo(ve)ment when a *not yet* becomes a *now here*.

Antigone prophetically makes ways *for* the future. She loosen(d)s enclosures, exposing them to what comes. She stands in thresholds, letting come.

Antigone survives, *for* the future. She prophesies *for* life, *for* the living, *for* the future.

A prophet is *for* the future. A prophet *for*-tells the future. A prophet stands between *already* and *not yet*. A prophet makes way *for* the future, and awaits its coming. A prophet then gives way to the future that comes.

Antigone goes further. She *for*-tells the future. She also performs a future. Her performance is her performative announcement of what is to come. She, prophetically, opens thresholds and then, angelically, passes through them.

Antigone announces the future by manifesting it. She announces the future that she is.

She is, *already*, *not yet*. She is both *already* and *not yet*. She comes, and keeps coming, *already* from the past and *not yet* from the future.

Antigone survives, persists, *for* sexual-animal-angelic-divine-humanity. She makes way, Judith Butler writes, for "its aberrant, unprecedented future."[14] She makes way for the "aberrant, unprecedented future" that she is. She perdures as future because her sexual-animal-angelic-divine-humanity is, though *already*, still *not yet*.

But in the present, Antigone is aberrant. She is aberrant in her sexuality, her human-animality, her divinity, her vitality, her temporality, her sustainability.

Antigone is aberrant. The future she is (*for*) is, too. It, as the future, is unprecedented. It is *encore*, and *à-venir*. It is queer. The future is a queer thing.[15]

Nothing disturbs like the future. The future is disturbing in unforeseeable ways. Queer is, too.

"Queer" is odd. It is not normal. It names, David Halperin writes, "whatever is at odds with the normal, the legitimate, the dominant. There is nothing in particular to which it necessarily refers. It is an identity without an essence . . . it designates a horizon of possibility whose precise extent and heterogeneous scope cannot in principle be delimited in advance."[16]

Queer is odd, and at odds. It is at odds with the normal, the legitimate, the dominant because they judge it odd. They except and exclude it. They expel and exile it. They do not exempt it, or excuse it, recognizing and respecting its differences.

Queer is odd, and at odds, because it resists. It resists renouncing its differences. It resists assimilation, sublation, incorporation. It resists. But resistance is not opposition.

Opposition is binary. The normal, the legitimate, the dominant are oppositional. (Kreon, representing this sovereign trinity, is oppositional.) On their accounting, differences do not count.

Resistance is plural. Queer resists being identified, judged, counted in this oppositional trinity's terms. It resists leaving no place for differences, for others, that remain different and other. It resists leaving no place for differences and others that are not yet delimited, or have not yet arrived. It resists leaving no possibilities for future differences and future others to come.

Opposition comes as *anti*. Resistance comes as *counter*.

(Antigone, I think, does not oppose Kreon. She resists him. She resists his edict. But he views her resistance as oppositional, and quells it.)

Queer resists, and its resistance can destabilize. Its *counter*-effects can destabilize, among other things, social and political order(s).

Queer signals a negativity, but one that is not simply negation. A queer negativity is like the negative. It maintains limits and limitations and finitude—and hence the future.

Queer names a counter-temporality. It, like Antigone, flows differently. It, like Antigone, opens and keeps open a space for resistance to come.

The future is a queer thing. So is Antigone. Antigone is future queer. (She is all kinds of queer.)

Antigone is queer *à-venir*. She is not "not yet queer." She is "queer not yet."

Queer is morphic. It has no essence. It has no essential nature. It has no necessary content or referent. It has no unbreakable bonds—not even sexual ones. Queer is sexual insofar as human-animals are sexual. But it is not only sexual. It is not a synonym for homosexual, or lesbian or gay, or transgender or intersex. Queer is not a sexual orientation. It is a dis-orientation, of more than sexuality.

(Antigone's sexualities would count as queer. Because *differences count*. And queer counts differently. It counts differences differently.)

Queer undoes. It loosen(d)s.

Queer is unnatural and unnaturalizing. It interrupts, disrupts, displaces. It destabilizes, disturbs. It shifts things. It gets things moving.

Queer is mobile. It moves. It is contextual. It *is* relational—like an angel.

Queer queries. It poses a question. Implicit in a queer question is the query "*what if* things were otherwise?"

Queer is questioning. It poses an open question. It interposes an interval, a threshold, a possible passage. It offers a potential for horizon(t)al transcendence.

Queer is an opening. It is open-ended. It remains not yet determined, not yet delimited. It has not yet arrived. Queer is not yet.[17]

Antigone, queer, is not yet. She has not yet arrived to stay. Her arrivals and rearrivals are temporary. She remains on the move, out of place, out of time. She comes from an other place, an other time.

She comes from past and future. She comes from ancient Athens, with her first casting in 442 BCE. She has since been recast and recast. But she remains *not yet*.

Antigone is not chrononormative. She is queerly temporal. Her counter-flows are temporal (as well as natural-cultural, species, sexual, spatial, maternal, ethical, vital). They are, in Elizabeth Freeman's words, "points of resistance to this temporal order that, in turn, propose other possibilities for living in relation to indeterminately past, present, and future others."[18] Temporal counter-flows affect relations. They affect the possibilities of relations. They reshape possible relations with others—others *not here, not now*. They reshape possible relations with the dead, with the living (proximate or distant), and with the *not yet*.

These queerly relational reshapings depend on differences and distances. They require respecting differences and distances, from others. They call for the negative.

Queer works the negative. The negative sustains differences. It demarcates and delimits. In doing so, it fashions thresholds. Thresholds are queer spaces. Queer comes in thresholds.

Antigone comes in a queerly temporal threshold. Hers is a threshold *of* the future (in both genitive senses). She moves through it in both directions: *to* the future and *from* the future. She comes-and-goes. She comes, but as *not yet*. She comes *and* remains *not yet*. She comes from the past *and* from the future—*and* remains future. She is still coming-and-going, through a future threshold.

Antigone arrives counter-temporally. She resists time's one-way flow, from future through present to past. She flows from the past, from the future, into the future. She juxtaposes disparate times, chiasmatically. She flows through temporal porosities.

Antigone delivers a queer counter-temporality. She delivers a counter-future. This counter-future never fully presents itself. It resists being delivered as a present. It resists being enveloped in a "present" identity. It is queerly resistant to presentation. It is persistently *not yet, not quite*.

With Antigone's queer counter-temporality comes her queer identity, which is also *not yet, not quite*. Queer, Gerald Loughlin writes, "seeks to outwit identity . . . to mark, and to make, a difference, a divergence."[19] Antigone's identity diverges, and diverges again. It is without an essence *and* without an envelope of identity. It is unessential, unenveloped. It is queerly porous, or porously queer.

Antigone's repeated returns, her coming-and-goings, her insistent futurity come from her queer counter-temporality. Her counter-temporal moves are *for* the future and *from* the future.

Antigone recasts the future, queerly. She recasts it erotically and subjectively, in her desire and her identity. She desires, and desires to be, *for* the future. She desires, and desires to be, *not yet*. Out of place, out of time, her *erōs* and her subjectivity perform Irigaray's appeal: "Let me go where I am *not yet*."[20]

This appeal is of the future. This appeal is of the future that Antigone is.

Antigone recasts the future differently, through differences of sexuality and species. She recasts it inter-actively, through spaces, times, relations.

She recasts it vitally, in terms of living risk. Her prophetic announcement calls for risk. She *for*-tells the risk of the future. She *for*-tells this future risk *for* life.

Antigone announces and is a risky future. She, Irigaray writes, senses "that if anything divine is still to come to us, it is in the abandon of all calculation. Of all language and all sense already produced. In risk. Only risk, of which no one knows where it leads. Of which future it is the announcement."[21] Antigone announces future risk. She *is* its announcement. She performs this announcement, as one of her performative roles.

Antigone lives on. She remains, as a question. She persists as a question of humanity, of the future. She insists as a question for humanity, for the future. She survives as a question of humanity *for* the future.

Antigone survives as a question of humanity in relation: with the living; with others, and other others; with animality and divinity; with pasts and futures.

Antigone survives as an open question, a querying threshold. She continues to question. She continues to ask *other* questions.

What about *others*? How do others count? How do they count among the living? How do they recount, revalue, who counts? How can their counting recount "us"?

What about *other* roles? What *other* roles will Antigone play? What *other* others will she enact? What other *counters* will she perform: other counter-humanities, counter-kinships, counter-temporalities? What will these *other* roles mean, in relation to others: vital, ethical, sexual, animal, divine, temporal? What futures will these *other* roles open and bring?

And how many *other* times will Antigone serve, once again, as a point of departure? How many *other* times will someone, reiterating Irigaray, "once again take the figure of Antigone as my point of departure"?[22]

What *other* questions will Antigone deliver?

Antigone remains an open question, without answer. Will her question, this question that she is, be answered? Will its answer come, once and for all?

How could it? Antigone comes from the past *and* from the future. She arrives as a question from the future for the future. She insists as a future question.

So these revivals are not Antigone's last. She remains horizonal. In her opening (on)to futurity, she remains open—at least half-way. She remains (in) an interval, a threshold. She awaits an other revival. She awaits other revivals, in the future.

I am—we are—not done with Antigone, not yet. I am—we are—undone with her. She remains, undoing and undone.

Notes

Previval

1. This allusion is to "Song of Myself" §51: "Do I contradict myself? / Very well then. . . . I contradict myself; / I am large. . . . I contain multitudes," where Whitman also writes, "The past and present wilt. . . . I have filled them and emptied them / And proceed to fill my next fold of the future." (These quotations are from the poem's original 1855 edition.)

2. These rereadings and reinterpretations are impossible to count. See the bibliography for a multidisciplinary sampling of readings that inform this text. For a catalog of Antigone's returns and revivals, her legacies and influences, see George Steiner, *Antigones* (New Haven, CT: Yale University Press, 1996).

3. See G. W. F. Hegel, *Phenomenology of Spirit*, trans. A. V. Miller (Oxford, UK: Oxford University Press, 1977), esp. ¶¶438–83; Martin Heidegger, *Introduction to Metaphysics*, trans. Gregory Fried and Richard Polt (New Haven, CT: Yale University Press, 2000), esp. 156–76; Jacques Lacan, *The Seminar of Jacques Lacan, Book VII: The Ethics of Psychoanalysis (1959–60)*, ed. Jacques-Alain Miller, trans. Dennis Porter (New York: Norton, 1992), esp. 241–87; Jacques Derrida, *Glas*, trans. John P. Leavey Jr. and Richard Rand (Lincoln: University of Nebraska Press, 1986), esp. 142–88; Judith Butler, *Antigone's Claim: Kinship Between Life and Death* (New York: Columbia University Press, 2000). This paragraph's quotations are from, respectively, Lacan, *Seminar VII*, 247; Derrida, *Glas*, 162; and Butler, *Antigone's Claim*, 82.

4. Luce Irigaray, *Thinking the Difference: For a Peaceful Revolution*, trans. Karin Morin (New York: Routledge, 1994), 70. Translation of *Le temps et la différence: Pour une révolution pacifique* (Paris: Livre de Poche, 1989), 84. Subsequent citations of Irigaray's (and others') texts give page

numbers from the English and then (when extant) the French editions. Here and throughout, I modify existing English translations for clarity and precision.

5. Irigaray, *Thinking the Difference*, 67/81; Luce Irigaray, *In the Beginning, She Was* (New York: Bloomsbury, 2013), 116. These revivals, Irigaray discloses in 2013, are philosophical and personal: "since *Speculum* and even before, I have been interested in Antigone. I have been fortunate enough . . . to experience exclusion because I tried to unveil truth, notably regarding Antigone" (*In the Beginning, She Was*, 114).

6. Luce Irigaray, *Democracy Begins Between Two*, trans. Kirsteen Anderson (New York: Routledge, 2000), 125. Translation of "Le question de l'autre," 40, in *De l'égalité des sexes* (Paris: Centre National de Documentation Pédagogique, 1995), 39–47. For related explorations of "other," see Luce Irigaray, *An Ethics of Sexual Difference*, trans. Carolyn Burke and Gillian C. Gill (Ithaca, NY: Cornell University Press, 1993), esp. 97–115; and Luce Irigaray, *I Love to You: Sketch of a Possible Felicity in History*, trans. Alison Martin (New York: Routledge, 1996), esp. 59–68. "Hommology," and later "hommosanguine," plays on "hommosexuality [*hommosexualité*]," a neologism Irigaray invents in *Speculum*. The supplementary *m* enfolds *homme*, a French word for "man," with *homo*, a Greek prefix for "same," a Latin word for "man," and the biological genus of humans. Sameness, *homo*, is sexed as masculine, *hommo*.

7. Sophokles, *Antigone*, trans. Ruby Blondell (Newburyport, MA: Focus, 1998), 376. Translation of Sophokles, *Antigone*, ed. Mark Griffith (Cambridge, UK: Cambridge University Press, 1999), 376. Citations of *Antigone* give line numbers that correspond in Greek and English. For a very different, very creative translation, see Sophokles, *Antigonick*, trans. Anne Carson, illus. Bianca Stone (New York: New Directions, 2012).

8. Luce Irigaray, "Belief Itself," 25, in *Sexes and Genealogies*, trans. Gillian C. Gill (New York: Columbia University Press, 1993), 23–53. Translation of *La croyance même* (Paris: Galilée, 1983), 13; and "La croyance même," 35, in *Sexes et Parentés* (Paris: Minuit, 1987), 35–65. For ease of reference, I cite all three texts in this order. But I work from the French text's earlier version, whose syntactic, signifying discontinuity I prefer. The plays between "*délié*" (literally, untied) and "*délibérément*" and between "*délibérément*" and "*librement*" are lost in translation.

9. Irigaray, "Belief Itself," 50/68/61–62.

10. Luce Irigaray, *This Sex Which Is Not One*, trans. Catherine Porter with Carolyn Burke (Ithaca, NY: Cornell University Press, 1985), 167.

Translation of *Ce Sexe qui n'en est pas un* (Paris: Minuit, 1977), 161. A more literal translation of this sentence might be "to stage the stakes of the work, I will redepart from the figure of Antigone."

11. Bonnie Honig, *Antigone, Interrupted* (Cambridge, UK: Cambridge University Press, 2013), 85.

12. Honig, *Antigone, Interrupted*, 89.

13. Irigaray, *This Sex Which Is Not One*, 167/161.

First Revival: Antigone the Animal

1. "Nature" also names a host of inorganic elements and phenomena, of chemical and physical events. They range from energy waves to ocean waves, from light to lightning, from sand to stars. But they form part of an ecological milieu in which living occurs. They affect and can be affected by living beings while remaining ungovernable by either.

2. Sophokles, *Antigone*, trans. Ruby Blondell (Newburyport, MA: Focus, 1998), 338–39, 342–46. I have considered the Ode to Man at length elsewhere (in *Trials: Of Antigone and Jesus* [New York: Fordham University Press, 2010], chap. 3).

3. Luce Irigaray, *Key Writings* (New York: Continuum, 2004), xiv. She continues: "Without working through this relation from the very beginning, we cannot succeed in entering into relation with all the kinds of other, not even with the same as ourselves." "From the very beginning" is ambiguous. It might mean working—from the very beginning of this working—through this relation. It might mean working through this relation from this relation's beginning. It might mean both. It would for Irigaray. It would for me, too, though only without an invisible, or unwritten, or silent "only" preceding "this relation." Such an invisible, or unwritten, or silent "only" seems to go without saying for Irigaray.

4. Here and throughout, I use "masculine" and "feminine" rather than "male" and "female." Earlier feminisms distinguished these terminal pairs by distinguishing gender from sex, culture from nature. I wish to blur rather than bolster these illusory distinctions. My preference for "masculine" and "feminine" is not a preference for gender or culture (or performativity) over sex or nature (or materiality). It is perhaps an idiosyncratic preference: "masculine" and "feminine" are existential and grammatical descriptors. They describe beings and words, and work across these domains.

5. Luce Irigaray, *An Ethics of Sexual Difference*, trans. Carolyn Burke and Gillian C. Gill (Ithaca, NY: Cornell University Press, 1993), 127. Translation of *Éthique de la différence sexuelle* (Paris: Minuit, 1984), 122.

6. Judith Butler, *Antigone's Claim: Kinship Between Life and Death* (New York: Columbia University Press, 2000), 41. See also Claude Lévi-Strauss, *The Elementary Structures of Kinship*, rev. ed., ed. Rodney Needham, trans. James Harle Bell and John Richard von Sturmer (Boston, MA: Beacon Press, 1969), esp. 24–25; Jacques Lacan, *The Seminar of Jacques Lacan, Book II: The Ego in Freud's Theory and in the Technique of Psychoanalysis (1954–1955)*, ed. Jacques-Alain Miller, trans. Sylvana Tomaselli (New York: Norton, 1991), esp. 29; Georges Bataille, *The Accursed Share*, vol. 2, *The History of Eroticism*, trans. Robert Hurley (New York: Zone Books, 1993), esp. 27–58; and Eve Kosofsky Sedgwick, *Tendencies* (Durham, NC: Duke University Press, 1993), esp. 5–9.

7. Luce Irigaray, *Speculum of the Other Woman*, trans. Gillian C. Gill (Ithaca, NY: Cornell University Press, 1985), 217. Translation of *Speculum, de l'autre femme* (Paris: Minuit, 1974), 270.

8. Queer, nonnormative, nonheteronormative, masculine sexualities can also emphasize kinship's materiality, in blood. But they do so by reimagining reproduction, not dematerializing it. (It is still a matter of blood, and of life and death.) They resexualize it, so that "reproduction" becomes "re-production," a kind of rebirth and kinship/sanguine reorientation, and so that paternity and maternity are no longer separable. Paternity and maternity become less important than genealogy (and immunology). Among gay men, this resexualizing also performs a fluid substitution: of (white) semen for (white) milk. See Leo Bersani and Adam Phillips, *Intimacies* (Chicago: University of Chicago Press, 2008); and Tim Dean, *Unlimited Intimacy: Reflections on the Subculture of Barebacking* (Chicago: University of Chicago Press, 2009).

9. "Blood rights [of mothers]," Irigaray writes, "are so completely neglected that 'consanguineous' is now defined as 'sired by the same father' and, what is more, set in opposition to the word 'uterine'" (*Speculum*, 125/157).

10. Luce Irigaray, *This Sex Which Is Not One*, trans. Catherine Porter with Carolyn Burke (Ithaca, NY: Cornell University Press, 1985), 77. Translation of *Ce Sexe qui n'en est pas un* (Paris: Minuit, 1977), 74.

11. Irigaray, *Speculum*, 221/275. This process is one, Irigaray describes here, in which blood "discolors in the proliferation of semblances, diversely exsanguine atoms of individual egos."

12. Irigaray, *Speculum*, 234/290.

13. She is not a human mother on Sophokles's account. But there are other accounts, other recountings, of other Antigones. On Euripides's account (by way of Alexander of Byzantium), Antigone is a mother. Euripides's *Antigone* diverges from Sophokles's *Antigone* in three key ways: (1) Kreon's guard discovers Haimon with Antigone at Polyneikes's (second) burial, (2) Haimon and Antigone are married, and (3) they have a son, Maeon. See J. H. Huddilston, "An Archaeological Study of the 'Antigone' of Euripides," *American Journal of Archaeology* 3 (1899): 183–201.

14. Rendering *anti* as *counter* makes way for Antigone's queer generation of and role in engendering feminine genealogies, which Irigaray details in *Thinking the Difference*, among other texts.

15. Luce Irigaray, *I Love to You: Sketch of a Possible Felicity in History*, trans. Alison Martin (New York: Routledge, 1996), 51. Translation of *J'aime à toi: Esquisse d'une félicité dans l'histoire* (Paris: Grasset, 1992), 91. The sexual difference inscribed in French by the parenthetical "e" is lost in translation.

16. Antigone performs her non-anti-maternity in her final speech, addressed to her tomb, which for her is both grave and marriage chamber. Interred by Kreon, she goes "unbedded, unaccompanied by wedding song, / without a share in marriage or the nurturing / of children" (Sophokles, *Antigone*, 917–19). Bonnie Honig considers maternalism and offers a reading of Antigone's dirge (one different from mine) in *Antigone, Interrupted* (Cambridge, UK: Cambridge University Press, 2013), 36–67 and 121–50.

17. Jacques Derrida, *Glas*, trans. John P. Leavey Jr. and Richard Rand (Lincoln: University of Nebraska Press, 1986), 150: "The whole analysis is fascinated by the essential figure of this sister who never becomes citizen, or wife, or mother. Dead before *being able to* get married, she fixes, grasps, transfixes, transfigures herself in this character of eternal sister, taking away with her her womanly, wifely desire" (my emphasis).

18. "Filial" and "feminine" each give two ways through sexual difference(s): sister-sister and sister-brother, and woman-woman and woman-man.

19. "To *all* her siblings" includes Ismene and Eteokles as well as Polyneikes. Antigone's ties to Polyneikes animate *Antigone*, given his body's pressing need for proper burial. Eteokles receives a proper burial, so Antigone's duty to him is filial but not pressing. What about Ismene? Does Antigone do her sisterly duty in relation to her sister? She tries to,

I think. She asks for Ismene's help in burying Polyneikes's body. Later she saves Ismene from Kreon's wrath and, so, from Antigone's punishment. Antigone and her actions are thoroughly bound by kinship ties. She is and acts relationally, and dutifully. When her relational duties conflict, she acts on behalf of those who cannot act for themselves (i.e., her dead brother, Polyneikes) rather than on behalf of those who can (i.e., her living sister, Ismene). Doing so does not mean she is a bad sister to Ismene. It does not mean she disavows her sisterly ties and duties. Simon Goldhill, Bonnie Honig, Mary Rawlinson, and Gail Schwab offer alternative readings of "the Ismene question."

20. Sophokles, *Antigone*, 466–68; see also 511: "I'm not ashamed of reverence for my flesh and blood."

21. Sophokles, *Antigone*, 909–14.

22. Valuing relation over individuality helps to allay castings of Antigone as "the lone individual," performing individuality and individualism, by standing up to "the man." This valuation suggests that Antigone acts less as "Antigone" than as "sister of Polyneikes-Eteokles-Ismene, daughter of Oedipus-Jokasta."

23. Sophokles, *Antigone*, 483–85; see also 678–80, where Kreon instructs Haimon, "by no means let a woman get the upper hand. / Better to fall, if we must do so, to a man; / then nobody could call us conquered by a woman."

24. Articulated differently, civic, hommosexual "kinship" is, for Kreon, a more important (and pretty queer) kind of kinship than familial kinship. Though Kreon acts to squelch blood bonds, he is the one who mentions "blood-bound" (*xunaimos*) three of the four times (198, 488, 659) it occurs in *Antigone*.

25. Sophokles, *Antigone*, 486–88. He adds: "nor will / her sister, her blood-kin, the other whom I hold / equally guilty in the planning of this tomb." For him, Ismene seems guilty by blood, not by deed.

26. Irigaray, *Speculum*, 225/280.

27. See Sophokles, *Antigone*, 35–36.

28. Irigaray, *Speculum*, 221/274.

29. See Sophokles, *Antigone*, 1220–22.

30. Sophokles, *Antigone*, 423–25.

31. Luce Irigaray, *Sexes and Genealogies*, trans. Gillian C. Gill (New York: Columbia University Press, 1993), 58. Translation of *Sexes et Parentés* (Paris: Minuit, 1987), 70.

32. Giorgio Agamben, *The Open: Man and Animal*, trans. Kevin Attell (Stanford, CA: Stanford University Press, 2004), 37; see also

33–38, 57–62, and 75–84. The open is a figure of Rainer Maria Rilke's (from his eighth Duino Elegy), which Martin Heidegger adopts and adapts, especially in terms of *alētheia*, or unconcealment. Agamben and Jean-Christophe Bailly return to this Heideggerian figure: Agamben more commentarially, Bailly more creatively.

33. Agamben, *The Open*, 77.

34. Agamben, *The Open*, 79.

35. Jacques Derrida, *The Animal That Therefore I Am*, ed. Marie-Louise Mallet, trans. David Wills (New York: Fordham University Press, 2008), 23. Translation of *L'Animal que donc je suis*, ed. Marie-Louise Mallet (Paris: Galilée, 2006), 54. This designation is enmeshed in hommohumanism. In its discourses on "the animal," Derrida writes, will appear "the same dominance, the same recurrence of a schema in truth invariable. What is it? The following: what is proper to man, his subjugating superiority over the animal, his very becoming-subject, his historicity, his emergence out of nature, his sociality, his access to knowledge and technics, all that, everything that constitutes (in a nonfinite number of predicates) what is proper to man would derive from this originary fault, indeed from this default in propriety, from what is proper to man as default in propriety" (*The Animal That Therefore I Am*, 45/70).

36. Derrida, *The Animal That Therefore I Am*, 47/73.

37. Butler, *Antigone's Claim*, 82.

38. Human-animal, and not humanimal. Why? The latter erases some humanity. Rather than entwining humanity and animality, inextricably, it collapses humanity into animality. For an implicit counterargument, see Kalpana Rahita Seshadri, *HumAnimal: Race, Law, Language* (Minneapolis: University of Minnesota Press, 2012), 21–22.

39. Matthew Calarco, *Zoographies: The Question of the Animal from Heidegger to Derrida* (New York: Columbia University Press, 2008), 3.

40. See Robert, *Trials*, 44–48. For other accounts of the posthuman, see Rosi Braidotti, *The Posthuman* (Malden, MA: Polity, 2013); N. Katherine Hayles, *How We Became Posthuman: Virtual Bodies in Cybernetics, Literature, and Informatics* (Chicago: University of Chicago Press, 1999); and Erin Manning, *Politics of Touch: Sense, Movement, Sovereignty* (Minneapolis: University of Minnesota Press, 2007).

41. Jean-Christophe Bailly, *The Animal Side*, trans. Catherine Porter (New York: Fordham University Press, 2011), 5. Translation of *Le versant animal* (Paris: Bayard, 2007), 15.

42. Bailly, *The Animal Side*, 5/16. "The contact," he writes, "is always vacillating; the encounter relates and even stipulates difference:

difference is there, it is there like an abyss, and this abyss is impassable" (*The Animal Side*, 5/15).

43. Irigaray, *Sexes and Genealogies*, 178/192.

44. See Jacques Derrida, *H. C. for Life, That Is to Say . . .* , trans. Laurent Milesi and Stefan Herbrechter (Stanford, CA: Stanford University Press, 2006), 88. Translation of *H. C. pour la vie, c'est à dire . . .* (Paris: Galilée, 2002), 78.

45. Bailly, *The Animal Side*, 46/92.

46. Derrida, *The Animal That Therefore I Am*, 31/53.

47. Jean-Christophe Bailly, "The Slightest Breath (On Living)," trans. Matthew H. Anderson, *CR: The New Centennial Review* 10, no. 3 (2011): 4. Translation of "Le moindre souffle (Sur le vivant)," 58–59, in *Le parti pris des animaux* (Paris: Christian Bourgois, 2013), 53–69.

48. "If respiration is the tangible and intimate form of living's exteriority to itself, or its extimacy (*extimité*), then nothing prevents one from imagining, describing, or comprehending the other porosities—all the protocols of exchange that make the widespread diversity of living possible" (Bailly, "The Slightest Breath (On Living)," 5/60).

49. Calarco, *Zoographies*, 106.

50. Bailly, "The Slightest Breath (On Living)," 3/55–56, 4/58.

51. Sophokles, *Antigone*, 29–30.

52. Judith Butler, *Precarious Life: The Powers of Mourning and Violence* (New York: Verso, 2004), xv and xx–xxi; see also 19–49, and Judith Butler, *Frames of War: When Is Life Grievable?* (New York: Verso, 2010), 1–23.

53. See Honig, *Antigone, Interrupted*, 68–82, for her interpretation of the 1978 film *Germany in Autumn*, which recasts Antigone as a gay German man, with former Nazis everywhere. For connections between Nazism and dehumanization, see Nicole Shukin, *Animal Capital: Rendering Life in Biopolitical Times* (Minneapolis: University of Minnesota Press, 2009).

54. Cary Wolfe, *Before the Law: Humans and Other Animals in a Biopolitical Frame* (Chicago: University of Chicago Press, 2013), 105. On a related note, Derrida discusses "a heterogeneous multiplicity of the living, more precisely (since to say 'the living' is already too much or not enough) a multiplicity of organizations of relations between the living and the dead" (*The Animal That Therefore I Am*, 31/53).

55. Bailly, *The Animal Side*, 44/89–90.

56. Sophokles, *Antigone*, 1001–02; see also 1005–22.

57. Sophokles, *Antigone*, 112–13.
58. Luce Irigaray, "Animal Compassion," trans. Marilyn Gaddis Rose, 198, in *Animal Philosophy*, ed. Peter Atterton and Matthew Calarco (New York: Continuum, 2004), 195–201.
59. Irigaray, "Animal Compassion," 197.
60. Irigaray, "Animal Compassion," 197.

Second Revival: Antigone the Angel

1. Sophokles, *Antigone*, trans. Ruby Blondell (Newburyport, MA: Focus, 1998), 850–52. Her displacement might be a-topic, or u-topic, or dis-topic, or some other-topic.
2. Luce Irigaray, *An Ethics of Sexual Difference*, trans. Carolyn Burke and Gillian C. Gill (Ithaca, NY: Cornell University Press, 1993), 51. Translation of *Éthique de la différence sexuelle* (Paris: Minuit, 1984), 55.
3. See Aristotle, *Physics*, trans. R. P. Hardie and R. K. Gaye, 211b14–19 and 212a13–20, in *The Complete Works of Aristotle*, vol. 1, ed. Jonathan Barnes (Princeton, NJ: Princeton University Press, 1984), 360–61.
4. Irigaray, *Ethics of Sexual Difference*, 51/55.
5. Jean-Luc Nancy, *L'Intrus* (Paris: Galilée, 2000), 11 (my translation).
6. See Sophokles, *Antigone*, 582–625; and Jacques Lacan, *The Seminar of Jacques Lacan, Book VII: The Ethics of Psychoanalysis (1959–60)*, ed. Jacques-Alain Miller, trans. Dennis Porter (New York: Norton, 1992), 262–83.
7. See Sophokles, *Antigone*, 1069–76.
8. Sophokles, *Antigone*, 2–4.
9. Sophokles, *Antigone*, 450–52.
10. Sophokles, *Antigone*, 453–55; see also 184, 304, 487, and 658.
11. Luce Irigaray, *In the Beginning, She Was* (New York: Bloomsbury, 2013), 120.
12. Luce Irigaray, *Key Writings* (New York: Continuum, 2004), 190; see also 149: "Religious is that which joins, links together. One of our actual religious tasks would be to find how to join earth and sky, body and soul or spirit, and even also cultures, sexes, and generations." This sense of "religious" entwines both possible etymologies of "religion": from *religere* (to gather together) and from *religare* (to bind).

13. See Luce Irigaray, *The Way of Love*, trans. Heidi Bostic and Stephen Pluháček (New York: Continuum, 2002), esp. 9, 140, 144–45, and 149; and Irigaray, *Key Writings*, 186–94.

14. Irigaray, *Ethics of Sexual Difference*, 82/84. This passage is difficult to translate. *Encore* can mean still, yet, even, further, again, anew. It can, in other words, signify endurance (still), anticipation (yet), intensification (even), extension (further), repetition (again), renewal (anew). This semantic range crisscrosses temporal and spatial senses in complex ways. Each semantic possibility significantly alters this phrase's meaning. There seems no good way to decide on one among them, so *encore* remains in play.

15. Irigaray, *Key Writings*, 148.

16. "Approaching the other thus requires a negative and nocturnal path, and the mystic love in part becomes a way for meeting together. Then it does not demand renouncing our sensibility or intelligence but agreeing with the fact that we cannot feel or know the all, especially in the world of the other" (Irigaray, *Key Writings*, 148).

17. Luce Irigaray, *Speculum of the Other Woman*, trans. Gillian C. Gill (Ithaca, NY: Cornell University Press, 1985), 201. Translation of *Speculum, de l'autre femme* (Paris: Minuit, 1974), 250.

18. Irigaray, *Ethics of Sexual Difference*, 129/124.

19. Irigaray, *Ethics of Sexual Difference*, 82/84. *Intermédiaire* can be a noun or an adjective. Here it remains undecidable.

20. Irigaray, *Ethics of Sexual Difference*, 129/124.

21. Luce Irigaray, "Belief Itself," 37, in *Sexes and Genealogies*, trans. Gillian C. Gill (New York: Columbia University Press, 1993), 23–53. Translation of *La croyance même* (Paris: Galilée, 1983), 41; and "La croyance même," 49, in *Sexes et Parentés* (Paris: Minuit, 1987), 35–65.

22. There is, Irigaray writes, "a danger if no third term exists. Not only to serve as a limitation. This third term can occur within the one who contains as a relation of the latter to his or her own limit(s): relation to the divine, to death, to the social, to the cosmic. If a third term does not exist within and for the container, he or she becomes *all-powerful*" (*Ethics of Sexual Difference*, 12/19).

23. Plato, *Timaeus*, trans. Peter Kalkavage (Newburyport, MA: Focus, 2001), 52b and 52e; see also 52d: "neither of the two comes to be in the other, neither will simultaneously become one and the same thing, and also two."

24. Irigaray, *Ethics of Sexual Difference*, 15/22.

25. They do so especially by being futural. Angels, Irigaray writes, "would circulate as mediators of that which has not yet happened, of what is still going to happen" (*Ethics of Sexual Difference*, 15/22).

26. Irigaray, *Ethics of Sexual Difference*, 7/15. She adds here that "it is necessary to reconsider the whole problematic of space and of time in order that this [sexual] difference take place in being thought and lived."

27. It also opens sexualities, sexual differences, and culture (or, perhaps, "culture"). It opens them to new possibilities, via new Antigones. See Luce Irigaray, *Elemental Passions*, trans. Joanne Collie and Judith Still (New York: Routledge, 1992), 3: "For this culture to advance, therefore, new models of sexual identity must be established."

28. See Irigaray, *Ethics of Sexual Difference*, 15/22.

29. See Irigaray, *I Love to You: Sketch of a Possible Felicity in History*, trans. Alison Martin (New York: Routledge, 1996), 109–28. Translation of *J'aime à toi: Esquisse d'une félicité dans l'histoire* (Paris: Grasset, 1992), 171–91. On mail carriers and postal systems, see Jacques Derrida, *The Post Card: From Socrates to Freud and Beyond*, trans. Alan Bass (Chicago: University of Chicago Press, 1987), esp. 411–96.

30. One of the most notable angelic announcements is Gabriel's annunciation to Mary of Mary's pregnancy. This annunciation is an explicitly sexual and corporeal announcement. It announces a counter-maternity: of a human-divine child. Irigaray discusses this annunciation in (among other places) *Marine Lover*, 171–72; *Ethics of Sexual Difference*, 15–16; *Sexes and Genealogies*, 36–38, 46, 62, and 70; *I Love to You* 123–24; *Way of Love*, 16; *To Be Two*, 54 (paired with Antigone); and *Key Writings*, 135 and 162–63.

31. Michel Serres, *Angels: A Modern Myth*, ed. Philippa Hurd, trans. Francis Cowper (Paris: Flammarion, 1995), 296.

32. For articulations of "cosmic," see Irigaray, *I Love to You*, 38, 94, 122–23, 135; and Irigaray, *Key Writings*, 23–24, 28, 64, 71, 101, 107–9, 134–36, 141, 151, 163, 168, 179, 202–5, 220, 252.

33. See Aristotle, *History of Animals*, trans. d'A. W. Thompson, 511b7, in *Complete Works of Aristotle*, vol. 1, 812; Aristotle, *Generation of Animals*, trans. A. Platt, 787b3, in *Complete Works of Aristotle*, vol. 1, 1216; and Rebecca Hill, *The Interval: Relation and Becoming in Irigaray, Aristotle, and Bergson* (New York: Fordham University Press, 2012), esp. 58–88. *Angeion* can also name body or placenta.

34. Aristotle, *Physics*, 209b29; see also 208b2–23 and 210a24.

35. Irigaray, *Ethics of Sexual Difference*, 16/22. Parousia, like advent, has become a technical term for Christianities. In Christian terms, parousia names a specific arrival: the rearrival, the second coming, of Christ at time's end. (Advent names a liturgical season of anticipating an arrival: the birth of Christ, celebrated as Christmas.) I use these terms in broader senses, not in these technical manners.

36. Perhaps a *parzousia*: *par* + *zoo* + *ousia*?

37. Irigaray, *Ethics of Sexual Difference*, 17/23.

38. "No thinking," Irigaray writes, "about sexual difference[s] that would not be traditionally hierarchical is possible without thinking through the mucous" (*Ethics of Sexual Difference*, 110/107).

39. Irigaray, *Ethics of Sexual Difference*, 110/107–08.

40. Irigaray, *Ethics of Sexual Difference*, 129/124.

41. See Christopher Cohoon, "Coming Together: The Six Modes of Irigarayan *Erōs*," *Hypatia* 26, no. 3 (2011): 478–96, esp. 483.

42. See Sophokles, *Antigone*, 90; and Robert, *Trials*, 6–35.

43. Irigaray, *Ethics of Sexual Difference*, 149/140.

44. Martin Heidegger also suggests a shift from theology to theiology. This shift would shift focus from *theos*, god, to *theios*, the divine. But Heidegger's shift does not evade ontotheology. Theology, for him, names a study of the highest being. Theology remains, in his terms, ontic. In my terms, though, theology would be released from an ontic envelope and opened as a way of coming to be.

45. Agnes Bosanquet, "Luce Irigaray's Sensible Transcendental: Becoming Divine in a Body," *Transformations* 11 (2005), http://www.transformationsjournal.org/journal/issue_11/article_01.shtml.

46. Irigaray, *Ethics of Sexual Difference*, 148/139–40, where she adds: "Waiting for parousia would require keeping all one's senses alert. Not destroyed, not covered, not 'dirtied,' our senses would be open. If God and the other are to be unveiled, I too must unveil myself."

47. Steven Chase, introduction to *Angelic Spirituality: Medieval Perspectives on the Ways of Angels*, ed. Steven Chase (Mahwah, NJ: Paulist Press, 2002), 61.

Third Revival: Antigone the Future

1. Sophokles, *Antigone*, trans. Ruby Blondell (Newburyport, MA: Focus, 1998), 519.

2. Sophokles, *Antigone*, 559–60. (I have interpreted this line differently elsewhere.)
3. Sophokles, *Antigone*, 814–16.
4. Sophokles, *Antigone*, 1019–21; see also 1001–11.
5. Sophokles, *Antigone*, 1067–71.
6. Sophokles, *Antigone*, 1064–67.
7. Luce Irigaray, *In the Beginning, She Was* (New York: Bloomsbury, 2013), 114.
8. It is, Irigaray writes, "the difficulty of unveiling the meaning of Antigone's will and act, and the resistance of our History to their realization, that explain why Antigone remains such a persistent myth in our tradition" (*In the Beginning, She Was*, 113).
9. Jacques Derrida, *H. C. for Life, That Is to Say . . .* , trans. Laurent Milesi and Stefan Herbrechter (Stanford, CA: Stanford University Press, 2006), 87. Translation of *H. C. pour la vie, c'est à dire . . .* (Paris: Galilée, 2002), 78.
10. Derrida, *H. C. for Life, That Is to Say . . .* , 87/78.
11. Luce Irigaray, "Belief Itself," 53, in *Sexes and Genealogies*, trans. Gillian C. Gill (New York: Columbia University Press, 1993), 23–53. Translation of *La croyance même* (Paris: Galilée, 1983), 76; and "La croyance même," 65, in *Sexes et Parentés* (Paris: Minuit, 1987), 35–65.
12. Roberto Esposito, *Third Person*, trans. Zakiya Hanafi (New York: Polity, 2012), 114.
13. Irigaray, "Belief Itself," 36/39/48.
14. Judith Butler, *Antigone's Claim: Kinship Between Life and Death* (New York: Columbia University Press, 2000), 82; see also 72.
15. For a very different reading of "queer" and "future," see Lee Edelman, *No Future: Queer Theory and the Death Drive* (Durham, NC: Duke University Press, 2004), esp. 102–09.
16. David M. Halperin, *Saint Foucault: Towards a Gay Hagiography* (Oxford, UK: Oxford University Press, 1995), 62. " 'Queer' seems," Eve Kosofsky Sedgwick writes, "to hinge much more radically and explicitly on a person's undertaking particular, performative acts of experimental self-perception and filiation" (*Tendencies*, 9).
17. See José Esteban Muñoz, *Cruising Utopia: The Then and New of Queer Futurity* (New York: New York University Press, 2009), 1 ("Queerness is not yet here. . . . Put another way, we are not yet queer."); 11 ("queerness is primarily about futurity and hope . . . queerness is always in the horizon"); 21 ("queerness is not quite here"); 22 ("we are not quite queer yet").

18. Elizabeth Freeman, *Time Binds: Queer Temporalities, Queer Histories* (Durham, NC: Duke University Press, 2010), xxii.

19. Gerald Loughlin, "The End of Sex," 9, in *Queer Theology: Rethinking the Western Body*, ed. Gerald Loughlin (Malden, MA: Blackwell, 2007), 1–34.

20. Luce Irigaray, *Elemental Passions*, trans. Joanne Collie and Judith Still (New York: Routledge, 1992), 25 (my emphasis). Translation of *Passions élémentaires* (Paris: Minuit, 1982), 30.

21. Irigaray, "Belief Itself," 53/76/65.

22. Luce Irigaray, *This Sex Which Is Not One*, trans. Catherine Porter with Carolyn Burke (Ithaca, NY: Cornell University Press, 1985), 167. Translation of *Ce Sexe qui n'en est pas un* (Paris: Minuit, 1977), 161.

Bibliography of Works Cited and Consulted

Abbott, Matthew. "The Animal for Which Animality Is an Issue." *Angelaki* 16, no. 4 (2011): 87–99.

Agamben, Giorgio. "Angels." Translated by Lorenzo Chiesa. *Angelaki* 16, no. 3 (2011): 117–23.

———. *Homo Sacer: Sovereign Power and Bare Life*. Translated by Daniel Heller-Roazen. Stanford, CA: Stanford University Press, 1998.

———. *The Open: Man and Animal*. Translated by Kevin Attell. Stanford, CA: Stanford University Press, 2004.

Ahmed, Sara. *Queer Phenomenology: Orientations, Objects, Others*. Durham, NC: Duke University Press, 2006.

———. "Happy Futures." In *The Promise of Happiness*, 160–98. Durham, NC: Duke University Press, 2010.

Anderson, Pamela Sue. "Transcendence and Feminist Philosophy: On Avoiding Apotheosis." In *Women and the Divine: Touching Transcendence*, edited by Gillian Howie and J'annine Jobling, 27–52. New York: Palgrave Macmillan, 2009.

Anderson, Sam. "The Inscrutable Brilliance of Anne Carson." *New York Times*, March 14, 2013.

Angelic Spirituality: Medieval Perspectives on the Ways of Angels. Edited by Steven Chase. Mahwah, NJ: Paulist Press, 2002.

Aristotle. *Generation of Animals*. Translated by A. Platt. In *The Complete Works of Aristotle*, edited by Jonathan Barnes, vol. 1, 1111–218. Princeton, NJ: Princeton University Press, 1984.

———. *History of Animals*. Translated by d'A. W. Thompson. In *The Complete Works of Aristotle*, edited by Jonathan Barnes, vol. 1, 774–993. Princeton, NJ: Princeton University Press, 1984.

———. *Physics*. Translated by R. P. Hardie and R. K. Gaye. In *The Complete Works of Aristotle*, edited by Jonathan Barnes, vol. 1, 315–446. Princeton, NJ: Princeton University Press, 1984.

Atterton, Peter, and Matthew Calarco, eds. *Animal Philosophy: Ethics and Identity*. New York: Continuum, 2004.

Bailly, Jean-Christophe. *The Animal Side*. Translated by Catherine Porter. New York: Fordham University Press, 2011. Originally published as *Le versant animal* (Paris: Bayard, 2007).

———. *Le parti pris des animaux*. Paris: Christian Bourgois, 2013.

———. "The Slightest Breath (On Living)." Translated by Matthew H. Anderson. *CR: The New Centennial Review* 10, no. 3 (2011): 1–12.

Bannet, Eve Tavor. "There Have to Be at Least Two." *Diacritics* 23, no. 1 (1993): 83–98.

Bataille, Georges. *The History of Eroticism*. Vol. 2 of *The Accursed Share*, translated by Robert Hurley. New York: Zone Books, 1993

Bennett, Larry J., and William Blake Tyrrell. *Recapturing Sophocles' "Antigone."* Lanham, MD: Rowman and Littlefield, 1998.

Bersani, Leo, and Adam Phillips. *Intimacies*. Chicago: University of Chicago Press, 2008.

Bonaventure of Bagnoregio. *The Journey of the Mind to God*. Translated by Philotheus Boehner. Edited by Stephen F. Brown. Indianapolis, IN: Hackett, 1993.

Bosanquet, Agnes. "Carnal Transcendence as Difference: The Poetics of Luce Irigaray." Ph.D. diss., Macquarie University, 2009.

———. "An Image Carnal and Divine: Angels Playing with Placentas." *Outskirts* 22 (2010), http://www.outskirts.arts.uwa.edu.au/volumes/volume-22/bosanquet.

———. "Luce Irigaray's Sensible Transcendental: Becoming Divine in a Body." *Transformations* 11 (2005), http://www.transformationsjournal.org/journal/issue_11/article_01.shtml.

———. "Seeking a Sensible Transcendental: An Amorous Exchange." *Outskirts* 14 (2006), http://www.outskirts.arts.uwa.edu.au/volumes/volume-14/bosanquet.

Boutang, Pierre, and George Steiner. *Dialogues: Sur le mythe d'Antigone, sur le sacrifice d'Abraham*. Paris: Jean-Claude Lattès, 1994.

Braidotti, Rosi. "The Politics of 'Life Itself' and New Ways of Dying." In *New Materialisms: Ontology, Agency, and Politics*, edited by Diana Coole and Samantha Frost, 201–18. Durham, NC: Duke University Press, 2010.

———. *The Posthuman*. Malden, MA: Polity, 2013.
Bruns, Gerald L. *On Ceasing to Be Human*. Stanford, CA: Stanford University Press, 2011.
Burke, Carolyn, Naomi Schor, and Margaret Whitford, eds. *Engaging with Irigaray*. New York: Columbia University Press, 1994.
Butler, Judith. *Antigone's Claim: Kinship Between Life and Death*. New York: Columbia University Press, 2000.
———. *Bodies That Matter: On the Discursive Limits of "Sex."* New York: Routledge, 1993.
———. *Frames of War: When Is Life Grievable?* New York: Verso, 2010.
———. *Precarious Life: The Powers of Mourning and Violence*. New York: Verso, 2004.
Calarco, Matthew. *Zoographies: The Question of the Animal from Heidegger to Derrida*. New York: Columbia University Press, 2008.
Canters, Hanneke, and Grace M. Jantzen. *Forever Fluid: A Reading of Luce Irigaray's Elemental Passions*. Manchester, UK: Manchester University Press, 2005.
Case, Sue-Ellen. *Feminist and Queer Performance: Critical Strategies*. New York: Palgrave Macmillan, 2009.
Casey, Damien. "Luce Irigaray and the Advent of the Divine: From the Metaphysical to the Symbolic to the Eschatological." *Pacifica* 12 (1999): 27–54.
Cavalieri, Paola. *The Death of the Animal: A Dialogue*. New York: Columbia University Press, 2009.
Cavell, Stanley, Cora Diamond, John McDowell, Ian Hacking, and Cary Wolfe. *Philosophy and Animal Life*. New York: Columbia University Press, 2008.
Chanter, Tina. "Antigone's Exemplarity: Irigaray, Hegel, and Excluded Grounds as Constitutive of Feminist Theory." In *Thinking With Irigaray*, edited by Mary C. Rawlinson, Sabrina L. Hom, and Serene J. Khader, 265–92. Albany: State University of New York Press, 2011.
———. *Ethics of Eros: Irigaray's Rewriting of the Philosophers*. New York: Routledge, 1995.
———. *Whose Antigone?: The Tragic Marginalization of Slavery*. Albany: State University of New York Press, 2011.
Chanter, Tina, and Sean D. Kirkland, eds. *The Returns of Antigone: Interdisciplinary Essays*. Albany: State University of New York Press, 2014.

Cimitile, Maria C., and Elaine P. Miller, eds. *Returning to Irigaray: Feminist Philosophy, Politics, and the Question of Unity*. Albany: State University of New York Press, 2007.

Cixous, Hélène. "Birds, Women, and Writing." In *Three Steps on the Ladder of Writing*, translated by Sarah Cornell and Susan Sellers, 111–20. New York: Columbia University Press, 1993.

Clark, David L. "Animals . . . In Theory: Nine Inquiries in Human and Nonhuman Life." *CR: The New Centennial Review* 11, no. 2 (2012): 1–16.

Clément, Catherine. "Jouissances: Between the Angel and the Placenta." In *Syncope: The Philosophy of Rapture*, translated by Sally O'Driscoll and Deirdre M. Mahoney, 200–16. Minneapolis: University of Minnesota Press, 1994.

Coetzee, J. M. *The Lives of Animals*. Edited by Amy Guttman. Princeton, NJ: Princeton University Press, 1999.

Cohoon, Christopher. "Coming Together: The Six Modes of Irigarayan Erōs." *Hypatia* 26, no. 3 (2011): 478–96.

Dean, Tim. *Unlimited Intimacy: Reflections on the Subculture of Barebacking*. Chicago: University of Chicago Press, 2009.

de la Durantaye, Leland. "The Suspended Substantive: On Animals and Men in Giorgio Agamben's 'The Open.'" *Diacritics* 33, no. 2 (2003): 3–9.

Derrida, Jacques. *The Animal That Therefore I Am*. Edited by Marie-Louise Mallet. Translated by David Wills. New York: Fordham University Press, 2008. Originally published as *L'Animal que donc je suis*, edited by Marie-Louise Mallet (Paris: Galilée, 2006).

———. "Avowing—The Impossible: 'Returns,' Repentance, and Reconciliation." Translated by Gil Anidjar. In *Living Together: Jacques Derrida's Communities of Violence and Peace*, edited by Elisabeth Weber, 18–41. New York: Fordham University Press, 2013.

———. *Glas*. Translated by John P. Leavey Jr. and Richard Rand. Lincoln: University of Nebraska Press, 1986.

———. *H. C. for Life, That Is to Say. . . .* Translated by Laurent Milesi and Stefan Herbrechter. Stanford, CA: Stanford University Press, 2006. Originally published as *H. C. pour la vie, c'est à dire. . . .* (Paris: Galilée, 2002).

———. *Khōra*. Translated by Ian McLeod. In *On the Name*, edited by Thomas Dutoit, 87–127. Stanford, CA: Stanford University Press, 1995.

———. *Of Hospitality: Anne Dufourmantelle Invites Jacques Derrida to Respond*. Translated by Rachel Bowlby. Stanford, CA: Stanford University Press, 2000.

———. *The Post Card: From Socrates to Freud and Beyond*. Translated by Alan Bass. Chicago: University of Chicago Press, 1987.

Deutscher, Penelope. "'The Only Diabolical Thing About Women . . .': Luce Irigaray on Divinity." *Hypatia* 9, no. 4 (1994): 88–111.

———. *A Politics of Impossible Difference: The Later Work of Luce Irigaray*. Ithaca, NY: Cornell University Press, 2002.

De Vries, Roland J. "With Luce Irigaray, Toward a Theology of Hospitality." *L'Esprit Créateur* 52, no. 3 (2012): 52–65.

Edelman, Lee. *No Future: Queer Theory and the Death Drive*. Durham, NC: Duke University Press, 2004.

Else, Gerald F. *The Madness of Antigone*. Heidelberg, DE: Carl Winter, 1976.

Esposito, Roberto. *Bíos: Biopolitics and Philosophy*. Translated by Timothy Campbell. Minneapolis: University of Minnesota Press, 2008.

———. *Terms of the Political: Community, Immunity, Biopolitics*. Translated by Rhiannon Noel Welch. New York: Fordham University Press, 2013.

———. *Third Person*. Translated by Zakiya Hanafi. Malden, MA: Polity, 2012.

Faulkner, Joanne. "Negotiating Vulnerability Through 'Animal' and 'Child': Agamben and Rancière at the Limit of Being Human." *Angelaki* 16, no. 4 (2011): 73–85.

Féral, Josette. "Antigone or the Irony of the Tribe." Translated by Alice Jardine and Tom Gora. *Diacritics* 8, no. 3 (1978): 2–14.

Foley, Helen P. "Antigone as Moral Agent." In *Tragedy and the Tragic*, edited by M. S. Silk, 49–73. Oxford, UK: Oxford University Press, 1996.

Freeman, Elizabeth. *Time Binds: Queer Temporalities, Queer Histories*. Durham, NC: Duke University Press, 2010.

Goldhill, Simon. "Antigone and the Politics of Sisterhood." In *Laughing with Medusa: Classical Myth and Feminist Thought*, edited by Vanda Zajko and Miriam Leonard, 141–62. Oxford, UK: Oxford University Press, 2006.

Gourgouris, Stathis. *Does Literature Think?: Literature as Theory for an Antimythical Era*. Stanford, CA: Stanford University Press, 2003.

Grosz, Elizabeth. *Irigaray and the Divine*. Sydney, AU: Local Consumption Publications, 1986.

———. "The Nature of Sexual Difference: Irigaray and Darwin." *Angelaki* 17, no. 2 (2012): 69–93.
Halperin, David M. *Saint Foucault: Towards a Gay Hagiography*. Oxford, UK: Oxford University Press, 1995.
Haraway, Donna. *The Companion Species Manifesto: Dogs, People, and Significant Otherness*. Chicago: Prickly Paradigm Press, 2003.
Hayles, N. Katherine. *How We Became Posthuman: Virtual Bodies in Cybernetics, Literature, and Informatics*. Chicago: University of Chicago Press, 1999.
Haynes, Patrice. "The Problem of Transcendence in Irigaray's Philosophy of Sexual Difference." In *New Topics in Feminist Philosophy of Religion: Contestations and Transcendence Incarnate*, edited by Pamela Sue Anderson, 279–96. New York: Springer, 2010.
Hegel, G. W. F. *Phenomenology of Spirit*. Translated by A. V. Miller. Oxford, UK: Oxford University Press, 1977.
Heidegger, Martin. *Introduction to Metaphysics*. Translated by Gregory Fried and Richard Polt. New Haven, CT: Yale University Press, 2000.
Henao Castro, Andrés Fabián. "Antigone Claimed: 'I Am a Stranger!' Political Theory and the Figure of the Stranger." *Hypatia* 28, no. 2 (2013): 307–22.
Hill, Rebecca. *The Interval: Relation and Becoming in Irigaray, Aristotle, and Bergson*. New York: Fordham University Press, 2012.
Hollywood, Amy. *Sensible Ecstasy: Mysticism, Sexual Difference, and the Demands of History*. Chicago: University of Chicago Press, 2002.
Hom, Sabrina Lea. "Antigone's Lament: Care, Death, and Subjectivity in Hegel and Irigaray." Ph.D. diss., Stony Brook University, 2009.
Honig, Bonnie. *Antigone, Interrupted*. Cambridge, UK: Cambridge University Press, 2013.
Huddilston, J. H. "An Archaeological Study of the Antigone of Euripides." *American Journal of Archaeology* 3 (1899): 183–201.
Ingram, Penelope. "From Goddess Spirituality to Irigaray's Angel: The Politics of the Divine." *Feminist Review* 66 (2000): 46–72.
———. *The Signifying Body: Towards an Ethics of Sexual and Racial Difference*. Albany: State University of New York Press, 2009.
Interrogating Antigone in Postmodern Philosophy and Criticism. Edited by S. E. Wilmer and Audronė Žukauskaitė. Oxford, UK: Oxford University Press, 2010.

Irigaray, Luce. "Animal Compassion." Translated by Marilyn Gaddis Rose. In *Animal Philosophy*, edited by Peter Atterton and Matthew Calarco, 195–201. New York: Continuum, 2004.

———. *La croyance même*. Paris: Galilée, 1983.

———. *Democracy Begins Between Two*. Translated by Kirsteen Anderson. New York: Routledge, 2000.

———. *Elemental Passions*. Translated by Joanne Collie and Judith Still. New York: Routledge, 1992. Originally published as *Passions élémentaires* (Paris: Minuit, 1982).

———. *An Ethics of Sexual Difference*. Translated by Carolyn Burke and Gillian C. Gill. Ithaca, NY: Cornell University Press, 1993. Originally published as *Éthique de la différence sexuelle* (Paris: Minuit, 1984).

———. *I Love to You: Sketch of a Possible Felicity in History*. Translated by Alison Martin. New York: Routledge, 1996. Originally published as *J'aime à toi: Esquisse d'une félicité dans l'histoire* (Paris: Grasset, 1992).

———. *In the Beginning, She Was*. New York: Bloomsbury, 2013.

———. *Key Writings*. New York: Continuum, 2004.

———. *Marine Lover of Friedrich Nietzsche*. Translated by Gillian C. Gill. New York: Columbia University Press, 1991. Originally published as *Amante marine, de Friedrich Nietzsche* (Paris: Minuit, 1980).

———. "La question de l'autre." In *De l'égalité des sexes*, edited by Michel de Manassein, 39–47. Paris: Centre National de Documentation Pédagogique, 1995.

———. *Sexes and Genealogies*. Translated by Gillian C. Gill. New York: Columbia University Press, 1993. Originally published as *Sexes et Parentés* (Paris: Minuit, 1987).

———. *Sharing the World*. New York: Continuum, 2008.

———. *Speculum of the Other Woman*. Translated by Gillian C. Gill. Ithaca, NY: Cornell University Press, 1985. Originally published as *Speculum, de l'autre femme* (Paris: Minuit, 1974).

———. *Thinking the Difference: For a Peaceful Revolution*. Translated by Karin Morin. New York: Routledge, 1994. Originally published as *Le temps et la différence: Pour une révolution pacifique* (Paris: Livre de Poche, 1989).

———. *This Sex Which Is Not One*. Translated by Catherine Porter with Carolyn Burke. Ithaca, NY: Cornell University Press, 1985. Originally published as *Ce Sexe qui n'en est pas un* (Paris: Minuit, 1977).

———. *The Way of Love*. Translated by Heidi Bostic and Stephen Pluháček. New York: Continuum, 2002.

———. *Why Different?: A Culture of Two Subjects*. Edited by Luce Irigaray and Sylvère Lotringer. Translated by Camille Collins. New York: Semiotext(e), 2000.

Jacobs, Carol. "Dusting Antigone." *MLN* 111, no. 5 (1996): 889–917.

Jones, Rachel. *Irigaray: Towards a Sexuate Philosophy*. Malden, MA: Polity, 2011.

Krier, Theresa, and Elizabeth D. Harvey, eds. *Luce Irigaray and Premodern Culture*. New York: Routledge, 2004.

Lacan, Jacques. *The Seminar of Jacques Lacan, Book II: The Ego in Freud's Theory and in the Technique of Psychoanalysis (1954–1955)*. Edited by Jacques-Alain Miller. Translated by Sylvana Tomaselli. New York: Norton, 1991.

———. *The Seminar of Jacques Lacan, Book VII: The Ethics of Psychoanalysis (1959–1960)*. Edited by Jacques-Alain Miller. Translated by Dennis Porter. New York: Norton, 1992.

Lacoue-Labarthe, Philippe. "The Caesura of the Speculative." In *Typography*, edited by Christopher Fynsk, 208–35. Stanford, CA: Stanford University Press, 1998.

Lawlor, Leonard. *This Is Not Sufficient: An Essay on Animality and Human Nature in Derrida*. New York: Columbia University Press, 2007.

Lévi-Strauss, Claude. *The Elementary Structures of Kinship*, rev. ed. Edited by Rodney Needham. Translated by James Harle Bell and John Richard von Sturmer. Boston, MA: Beacon Press, 1969.

Loraux, Nicole. *Tragic Ways of Killing a Woman*. Translated by Anthony Forster. Cambridge, MA: Harvard University Press, 1991.

Loughlin, Gerald. "The End of Sex." In *Queer Theology: Rethinking the Western Body*, edited by Gerald Loughlin, 1–34. Malden, MA: Blackwell, 2007.

MacCormack, Patricia. "Mucous, Monsters, and Angels: Irigaray and Zulawski's 'Possession.'" *Cinema: Journal of Philosophy and the Moving Image* 1 (2010): 95–110.

Mader, Mary Beth. "Antigone and the Ethics of Kinship." In *Rewriting Difference: Luce Irigaray and 'The Greeks,'* edited by Elena Tzelepis and Athena Athanasiou, 93–104. Albany: State University of New York Press, 2010.

Manassein, Michel de, ed. *De l'égalité des sexes*. Paris: Centre National de Documentation Pédagogique, 1995.

Manning, Erin. *Politics of Touch: Sense, Movement, Sovereignty*. Minneapolis: University of Minnesota Press, 2007.
Martin, Alison. *Luce Irigaray and the Question of the Divine*. London: Modern Humanities Research Association, 2000.
Meltzer, Françoise. "Theories of Desire: Antigone Again." *Critical Inquiry* 37, no. 2 (2011): 169–86.
Michau, Michael R. "Antigone's Work(s) of Love." *New Antigone* 1 (2005): 58–66.
Miller, Elaine P. "The 'Paradoxical Displacement': Beauvoir and Irigaray on Hegel's Antigone." *Journal of Speculative Philosophy* 14, no. 2 (2000): 121–37.
Muñoz, José Esteban. *Cruising Utopia: The Then and Now of Queer Futurity*. New York: New York University Press, 2009.
Nancy, Jean-Luc. *L'Intrus*. Paris: Galilée, 2000.
Neuburg, Matt. "How Like a Woman: Antigone's 'Inconsistency.'" *Classical Quarterly* 40 (1990): 54–76.
Oliver, Kelly. *Animal Lessons: How They Teach Us to Be Human*. New York: Columbia University Press, 2009.
Oudemans, Th. C. W., and A. P. M. H. Lardinois. *Tragic Ambiguity: Anthropology, Philosophy, and Sophocles' "Antigone."* Leiden, NL: Brill, 1987.
Pini, Giorgio. "The Individuation of Angels from Bonaventure to Duns Scotus." In *A Companion to Angels in Medieval Philosophy*, edited by Tobias Hoffman, 79–115. Leiden, NL: Brill, 2012.
Plato. *Timaeus*. Translated by Peter Kalkavage. Newburyport, MA: Focus, 2001.
Porphyry. *On Abstinence from Killing Animals*. Translated by Gillian Clark. Ithaca, NY: Cornell University Press, 2000.
Pritchard, Annie. "Antigone's Mirrors: Reflections on Moral Madness." *Hypatia* 7, no. 3 (1992): 77–93.
Pseudo-Dionysius. *Complete Works*. Translated by Colm Luibhéid with Paul Rorem. Mahwah, NJ: Paulist Press, 1987.
Purvis, Jennifer. "Generations of Antigone: An Intra-Feminist Dialogue with Beauvoir, Irigaray, and Butler." *New Antigone* 1 (2005): 2–10.
Queer Times, Queer Becomings. Edited by E. L. McCallum and Miko Tuhkanen. Albany: State University of New York Press, 2011.
Rawlinson, Mary C., Sabrina L. Hom, and Serene J. Khader, eds. *Thinking with Irigaray*. Albany: State University of New York Press, 2011.
Robert, William. "Antigone's Nature." *Hypatia* 25, no. 2 (2010): 412–36.

———. "Human, Life, and Other Sacred Stuff." *Journal for Cultural and Religious Theory* 10, no. 1 (2009): 64–80.

———. *Trials: Of Antigone and Jesus.* New York: Fordham University Press, 2010.

Segal, Charles. "Sophocles' Praise of Man and the Conflict of the Antigone." *Arion* 3, no. 2 (1964): 46–66.

Serres, Michel. *Angels: A Modern Myth.* Edited by Philippa Hurd. Translated by Francis Cowper. Paris: Flammarion, 1995.

Seshadri, Kalpana Rahita. *HumAnimal: Race, Law, Language.* Minneapolis: University of Minnesota Press, 2012.

Schwab, Gail M. "Beyond the Vertical and the Horizontal: Spirituality, Space, and Alterity in the Work of Luce Irigaray." In *Thinking With Irigaray*, edited by Mary C. Rawlinson, Sabrina L. Hom, and Serene J. Khader, eds., 77–97. Albany: State University of New York Press, 2011.

———. "Mothers, Sisters, and Daughters: Luce Irigaray and the Female Genealogical Line in the Stories of the Greeks." In *Rewriting Difference: Luce Irigaray and "The Greeks,"* edited by Elena Tzelepis and Athena Athanasiou, 79–92. Albany: State University of New York Press, 2010.

Sedgwick, Eve Kosofsky. *Tendencies.* Durham, NC: Duke University Press, 1993.

Shukin, Nicole. *Animal Capital: Rendering Life in Biopolitical Times.* Minneapolis: University of Minnesota Press, 2009.

Sjöholm, Cecilia. *The Antigone Complex: Ethics and the Invention of Feminine Desire.* Stanford, CA: Stanford University Press, 2004.

Söderbäck, Fanny, ed. *Feminist Readings of Antigone.* Albany: State University of New York Press, 2010.

Sophokles. *Antigone.* Translated by Ruby Blondell. Newburyport, MA: Focus, 1998.

———. *Antigone.* Edited by Mark Griffith. Cambridge, MA: Cambridge University Press, 1999.

———. *Antigonick.* Translated by Anne Carson. Illustrated by Bianca Stone. New York: New Directions, 2012.

Steeves, H. Peter, ed. *Animal Others: On Ethics, Ontology, and Animal Life.* Albany: State University of New York Press, 1999.

Steiner, George. *Antigones.* New Haven, CT: Yale University Press, 1996.

Still, Judith. "Sharing the World: Luce Irigaray and the Hospitality of Difference." *L'Esprit Créateur* 52, no. 3 (2012): 40–51.

Tilghman, Carolyn M. "The Flesh Made Word: Luce Irigaray's Rendering of the Sensible Transcendental." *Janus Head* 11, no. 1 (2009): 39–54.

Tzelepis, Elena, and Athena Athanasiou, eds. *Rewriting Difference: Luce Irigaray and "The Greeks."* Albany: State University of New York Press, 2010.

Vernant, Jean-Pierre, and Pierre Vidal-Naquet. *Myth and Tragedy in Ancient Greece*. Translated by Janet Lloyd. New York: Zone Books, 1990.

Walsh, Keri. "Antigone Now." *Mosaic* 41, no. 3 (2008): 1–13.

Walsh, Lisa. "Her Mother Her Self: The Ethics of the Antigone Family Romance." *Hypatia* 14, no. 3 (1999): 96–125.

Weil, Kari. *Thinking Animals: Why Animal Studies Now?* New York: Columbia University Press, 2012.

Weil, Simone. *Intimations of Christianity Among the Ancient Greeks*. New York: Routledge, 1998.

Whitford, Margaret. *Luce Irigaray: Philosophy in the Feminine*. New York: Routledge, 1991.

Wolfe, Cary. *Before the Law: Humans and Other Animals in a Biopolitical Frame*. Chicago: University of Chicago Press, 2013.

Zeitlin, Froma. "Thebes: Theater of Self and Society in Athenian Drama." In *Nothing to Do with Dionysos?*, edited by John J. Winkler and Froma I. Zeitlin, 130–67. Princeton, NJ: Princeton University Press, 1990.

Zoontologies: The Question of the Animal. Edited by Cary Wolfe. Minneapolis: University of Minnesota Press, 2003.

INDEX

Agamben, Giorgio, 14, 15, 76–77n32, 77nn33–34
angel, xvi, xvii, xx, 31, 33, 45–58, 59–60, 62–64, 66, 81n25, 81n30
animal, xvi, xvii, xix, xx, 1, 2, 4, 12–26, 28–29, 31, 36, 44, 46, 59, 63, 64, 69, 77n35, 77n38
animal-divine, 46, 47
annunciation, 81n30
anthropological machine, 14–17, 19, 20, 27
anti, 6–7, 65, 75n14
antihumanism, xiii, xvii, 20
Antigone, xi–xxi, 1, 2, 5–23, 26–31, 33–39, 44–46, 49–50, 54–55, 58, 59–69, 71n2, 72n5, 72–73n10, 75nn13–14, 75n16, 75–76n19, 76n22, 78n53, 81n27, 81n30, 83n8
Aristotle, 51, 79n3, 81n33
augury, 29–31, 46, 60, 61

Bailly, Jean-Christophe, 20–21, 24, 25, 29, 76–77n32, 78n48
Bataille, Georges, 74n6

Bersani, Leo, 74n8
between, xx–xxi, 7, 8, 15, 21, 25, 33, 34, 39, 40, 42, 44–47, 50, 53–54, 62
biopolitics, xvii, xix, 26–28
bios, 25–28
bird, 2, 13–14, 17, 21, 22, 26, 28–31, 33, 36, 38, 46, 61
birth, xx, 6, 7, 24, 28, 34, 35, 40–43, 45–47, 74n8, 82n35
blood, xii, 1, 2, 4–6, 8–9, 11–13, 23, 24, 27–30, 37, 45, 51, 54, 61, 63, 74nn8–9, 74n11, 76n20
body, xv, 5, 9, 13, 29–31, 34, 37, 38, 40, 45, 51, 53, 55, 75–76n19, 79n12, 81n33
Bosanquet, Agnes, 56
Braidotti, Rosi, 77n40
breath, xix, 24, 28, 31, 42, 50, 51, 56
breathe, 5, 6, 21, 24–25, 35, 41, 42, 45, 53, 58, 63
brother, xv, 5, 9–10, 30, 31, 37, 75n18, 75–76n19
burial, xv, 11, 14, 30, 37, 38, 61, 75n13

Butler, Judith, xiii, 4, 18, 27, 64

Calarco, Matthew, 18, 25
Carson, Anne, xi
Cohoon, Christopher, 82n41
corporeal, xix, 4, 5, 12, 24, 34, 40–45, 49, 51–58, 63, 81n30
counter, 7, 34, 65, 69, 75n14
counter-humanity, 18, 20, 28, 63, 69
counter-kinship, 23–24, 28, 31, 69
counter-maternity, 8, 9, 47, 54, 63
counter-temporality, 66–69
culture, xiv, 1–7, 11, 18, 26, 33, 73n4, 79n12, 81n27

dead, the, xiv, 1, 23–26, 28, 36, 37, 44, 46, 50, 60, 63, 67, 78n54
death, xiii, 1, 4, 9, 12, 13, 23–28, 30, 31, 35, 37, 41, 60, 61, 74n8, 80n22
Dean, Tim, 74n8
Derrida, Jacques, xiii, 1, 8, 16, 24, 62–63, 75n17, 77n35, 78n44, 78n54, 81n29
desire, xiii, xv, 3, 5, 23, 27, 33, 37, 44, 54, 61, 63, 68, 75n17
divine, xiv, xv, xvii, xx–xxi, 14, 30, 34, 36–38, 43–47, 49–52, 54, 56–58, 60–61, 63, 64, 68, 69, 80n22, 81n30, 82n44
divinity, 30, 44–46, 55–57, 65

Edelman, Lee, 83n15
envelope, 48–52, 55–58, 67–68, 82n44
erōs, 55, 68
Esposito, Roberto, 33, 63

Eteokles, xv, 13, 30, 37, 60, 75n19, 76n22
ethics, xiv, xviii, 25, 42–45, 48, 49, 51, 53, 55, 57
Eurydike, xv, 13, 27
exception, 14–15, 55

feminanimal, 22–24, 27–29, 36, 63
feminine, xiii–xv, 3, 5–7, 9–11, 16, 17, 21–22, 33–34, 46, 73n4, 75n14, 75n18
femininity, 5, 7, 8, 12–14, 33, 63
filial, xv, 8–10, 13, 28, 29, 33, 37, 61, 75nn18–19
filial-feminine, 7–13, 15, 17, 28, 54
fluid, 3–7, 9, 11–14, 17, 29, 33, 34, 54, 55, 74n8
flow, xii, 1, 2, 4, 6–14, 17–18, 20, 22–24, 28, 33–35, 37, 42, 45–47, 49–50, 66–67
Freeman, Elizabeth, 67
future, xvi, xvii, xx, 29–30, 55, 58, 59–69, 71n1, 83n15

genealogy, xiv, xvi, 39, 55, 74n8, 75n14
god, 37, 38, 44, 45, 47, 49, 50, 54, 56–57, 60, 82n44
goddess, 46, 56, 60
gods, xii, 2, 22, 30, 31, 36–39, 44, 45, 47, 48, 50, 51, 61
Goldhill, Simon, 75–76n19

Hades, 10, 37, 38, 60, 61
Haimon, xv, 13, 27, 37, 61, 75n13, 76n23
Halperin, David, 65

Hayles, Katherine, 77n40
Hegel, G.W.F., xiii, 7, 8
Heidegger, Martin, xiii, 76–77n32, 82n44
Hill, Rebecca, 81n33
hommohumanism, 2, 7, 8, 10, 12–17, 19–20, 23, 29, 31, 38, 49, 55, 63
hommosexuality, 2, 6–8, 11, 15, 34, 43, 72n6, 76n24
Honig, Bonnie, xx, 75n16, 75–76n19, 78n53
Huddilston, J.H., 75n13
human, xiii, xvi–xviii, xx–xxi, 1–5, 13–22, 26–31, 33, 36, 37, 44–47, 51, 54, 57, 63, 72n6, 75n13
human-animal, xvii, xx, 17–21, 28, 29, 31, 36, 38, 44, 45, 48–53, 55, 64–66, 77n38
human-divine, xvii, xx, 36, 44, 45, 81n30
humanism, xvii, 2–6, 12, 14–20, 26, 28, 77n35
humanity, 9, 17–22, 30, 31, 57, 64, 68–69, 77n38
hyphen, 4, 5, 7, 8, 18, 20, 21, 35, 36, 46

incest, xv, 4–5, 12, 31, 37
inhuman, xiii, xv–xvii, 12, 17, 20, 28
inter-, xxi, 17, 21, 35, 36, 48, 59, 62
interact, 34–36, 39, 42–44, 53, 56–58
interscendence, 40
interval, 17, 34–40, 42–53, 55–58, 62, 63, 66, 69

Irigaray, Luce, xiii–xv, xviii–xx, 1, 3–8, 11–12, 14, 22–23, 31, 33–35, 39–40, 43–44, 47–48, 52–54, 56–57, 59, 62–64, 68–69, 72n6, 73n3, 74n9, 74n11, 75n14, 80n13, 80n16, 80n22, 81nn25–30, 81n32, 82n38, 83n8
Ismene, xv, 37, 60, 75–76n19

Jokasta, xv, 5, 37, 76n22

khōra, 47
kinship, xiii, xv, 2, 4–6, 9–11, 13–14, 17, 18, 23–24, 28, 29, 31, 37, 74n8, 75–76n19, 76n24
Kreon, xv, 9–14, 26–30, 37–38, 49, 60–61, 65, 75n13, 75n16, 75–76n19, 76nn23–24

Lacan, Jacques, xiii, 74n6, 79n6
Lévi-Strauss, Claude, 74n6
life, xiii, xiv, xix, xxi, 1, 4, 13, 23, 25–28, 31, 36, 37, 41, 45, 53, 58, 63, 64, 68, 74n8
limit, xvi, 7–8, 16, 20, 21, 24, 34, 35, 37, 39–40, 43, 66, 80n22
living, xii, xiv, xxi, 2, 3, 5, 11, 12, 17, 22–26, 28, 30, 33, 35–37, 40–46, 48, 51–54, 56–58, 61, 63, 67, 68, 73n1, 75–76n19, 78n48
living, the, xxi, 1, 16, 23–26, 28, 37, 39, 44, 46, 50, 56, 58, 60, 63, 64, 67, 69, 78n54
loosen(d), xviii, xix, xxi, 3, 17, 21, 34, 40, 43, 49, 57, 64, 66
Loughlin, Gerald, 68
love, xiv, 7, 31, 34, 50, 80n16

Manning, Erin, 77n40
material, xi, xix, 4–5, 24, 25, 28, 34, 41, 42, 52, 54
materiality, 4–6, 54, 73n4
maternal, 5–6, 9–11, 17, 28–29, 33, 67, 75n16
maternalfeminine, 5–10, 14, 15, 47, 50
maternity, 5, 7–10, 63, 74n8, 75n16
miasma, 12, 27
milk, 6, 8, 9, 29, 54, 74n8
mother, 5–10, 13, 29, 31, 46, 74n9, 75n13, 75n17
mother bird, 13, 14, 28–31, 33, 38
mourning, 31
mucous, 53–54, 57, 63, 82n38
Muñoz, José, 59, 83n17
mystical, 43

Nancy, Jean-Luc, 36
nature, 1–4, 6, 7, 11, 16, 26, 33, 66, 73n1, 77n35
nature-culture, 4, 6, 7, 12, 13, 22
negative, the, 7–8, 21, 34, 37, 40–43, 57, 66, 67
not yet, 19, 34, 52, 55, 62–69, 81n25, 83n17

Oedipus, xv, 5, 37, 76n22
oikos, xiii, 6, 33, 37
ontology, xiv, xvii–xix, xxi, 3, 22, 24, 28, 42, 43, 52
other, xiii–xxi, 1, 2, 6–8, 11, 13–17, 22, 24–27, 31, 33–37, 39–44, 47–49, 52, 56–58, 60, 63, 65, 67, 69, 72n6, 73n3, 80n16, 82n46

parousia, 52–58, 64, 82n35, 82n46
passage, 15, 17, 24, 25, 34–40, 42, 44–46, 48–54, 57, 58, 63–64, 66
paternalmasculine, 6, 10, 15, 50
Phillips, Adam, 74n8
piety, xv, 9, 37, 61
plant, 22, 25
Plato, 47, 80n23
polis, 11, 33
poly, xii, xvi, 26, 48, 50, 57
Polyneikes, xv, 9–11, 13, 26, 27, 29–31, 37–39, 60, 61, 75n13, 75–76n19, 76n22
polyzoontic, xii
polyzoontopolitics, 26, 28, 63
porosity, 17, 24–26, 28
porous, 17, 24–25, 34, 46, 57, 68
posthuman, xvii, xix, 17, 19–20, 77n40
prophet, 29–30, 59–64, 68
proximity, 4, 24, 35, 40, 43, 44, 49, 52, 53, 67

queer, xix, 59, 65–68, 74n8, 75n14, 76n24, 83nn15–17

Rawlinson, Mary, 75–76n19
relation, xv, xvii, xx–xxi, 1, 4, 7–10, 18, 19, 21, 23–26, 28, 30, 31, 35, 36, 39–43, 45–49, 51, 52, 54–57, 59, 63, 66–69, 73n3, 75n19, 76n22, 78n54, 80n22
religion, xii, xv, 30, 36–37, 39, 43, 45, 79n12
reproduction, xvi, 5, 74n8
revival, xiii, xiv, xvi–xxi, 14, 34, 41, 44–45, 62, 69, 71n2, 72n5

risk, xix–xx, 3–4, 9, 10, 19, 68

sanguine, 4, 6, 8–9, 11–13, 29, 33, 54, 74nn8–9, 74n11
sensible transcendence, 40–45, 49, 50, 51, 54–56, 58, 64
Serres, Michel, 51
Seshadri, Kalpana, 77n38
sexual difference(s), xiv, 2–3, 7–9, 11, 12, 22–23, 54, 63, 75n15, 81n27, 82n38
sexuality, 6, 7, 11, 14–16, 19, 21–23, 28, 33, 34, 52, 55, 58, 63, 65, 66, 68
Schwab, Gail, 75–76n19
Sedgwick, Eve Kosofsky, 74n6, 83n16
sister, xiii, xv, 8–9, 11, 13, 31, 33, 37, 54, 75nn17–18, 75–76n19, 76n22, 76n25

Shukin, Nicole, 78n53
Sophokles, xvi, 2, 13, 29, 60, 75n13, 76n27, 76n29, 79nn6–7, 82n42
Steiner, George, 71n2
subjectivity, 8, 37, 55, 68

Teiresias, 30, 60–61
thanatos, 25, 26
theiology, 56, 82n44
theology, 56, 82n44
threshold, xxi, 34–37, 39, 40, 43–46, 51–56, 58, 62–64, 66, 67, 69
transcendence, 4, 37, 39–42, 44, 45

Wolfe, Cary, 28

Zeus, 11, 37–38, 46, 61
zōē, xii, 25, 26, 28

www.ingramcontent.com/pod-product-compliance
Ingram Content Group UK Ltd.
Pitfield, Milton Keynes, MK11 3LW, UK
UKHW041855111225
465990UK00015B/93